Splendors of Ancient Egypt

Splendors of Ancient Egypt

From the
Egyptian Museum
Cairo
written and
compiled by
Dr. Robert S. Bianchi

**Presented by
Florida International Museum
St. Petersburg**

Booth-Clibborn Editions
London

Previous page
A view of the Giza Plateau
Whenever one thinks about ancient
Egypt, the Great Pyramids and Sphinx
on the Giza Plateau immediately
spring to mind. Throughout the ages
these massive structures have
fascinated, mystified, and enchanted
all those who have stood in awe
before them. Indeed, the Great
Pyramids are the only example of the
Seven Wonders of the Ancient World
to have survived intact to this day.
It is no wonder, then, that an ancient
proverb proclaims, "Mankind fears
Time, but Time fears the Pyramids!"
Built not by slaves, but by free
members of Egyptian society, as
revealed by recent reinvestigations
of the village in which those laborers
lived when they toiled away on these
massive construction projects, the
pyramids are the final resting places –
massive sepulchers – of some of the
mightiest rulers ever to have lived
on earth. Within the relieving
compartments of the Grand Gallery
of the Pyramid of Kufu are the
remains of inscriptions, termed quarry
marks, painted in black ink by the
overseers responsible for obtaining the
stone. These inscriptions record
that the Great Pyramid was intended
for Kufu, whose name they contain.
The ancient Egyptians also named
each pyramid, and called this one
"The Horizon of Kufu."
The Great Sphinx crouches as an
eternal sentinel, symbolically poised
to ward off any evil approaching these
mighty tombs. Recent popular
attempts in television programs and
the print media to redate the Sphinx
to an earlier period and to attribute
it to a culture even earlier than Egypt
are based on a symbolist
interpretation of ancient Egyptian
culture, whose proponents cling
to their theories with a quasi-religious
zeal. The Great Sphinx was erected
by command of Khaefre, for whom
the second pyramid on the plateau
served as a sepulcher. They named his
pyramid, "Great is Khaefre."

Author: Dr. Robert S. Bianchi

Art Director: David Hillman
Design: Anna-Lisa Schönecker,
Pentagram Design

Editor: Mark Sutcliffe

Photographer: Phil Sayer

Copyright ©
The Egyptian Museum, Cairo
Copyright ©
Broughton International Inc.
Text copyright ©
Dr. Robert S. Bianchi
Photography copyright © Phil Sayer

First published in 1996 by
Booth-Clibborn Editions
12 Percy Street,
London W1P 9FB
Cover illustration: View of the
Giza Plateau
ISBN: 1873968 914

Printed by Mondadori, Italy

CONTENTS

10

Previous page
A view of the Nile River from Luxor toward Western Thebes
Herodotus, the Father of History, writing in Greek about 450 B.C., remarked that Egypt was the gift of the Nile. From his vantage the annual flooding of the Nile, caused by the rains and melting snows of the highlands of Central Africa, left a thin, rich deposit of alluvial soil on the Egyptian flood plain which could be easily worked by the farmers. The warm, nurturing Egyptian sun and the ready supply of water for irrigation in the Nile itself contributed to the abundance of crops grown, particularly of grain. As a result, Egypt was called the bread basket of the world.
The Nile River was also the country's principal highway. In antiquity the Egyptians readily traveled from one end of their country to the other on the river. They were also shuttled back and forth between its banks. Things have not changed. Even today, here at Thebes vessels shuttle tourists back and forth between Luxor, located on the east bank, and the bank of Western Thebes. In many ways, Herodotus' remark is as true today as it was when he first made it. True, the Nile no longer floods its banks annually as it did in antiquity because of the construction of the Aswan High Dam which became functional on January 15, 1971. Nevertheless, humanitarians worldwide agree that the waters backed up behind that dam which form Lake Nasser constitute an important reservoir. As a result, the modern peoples of both Egypt and The Sudan have not suffered in recent years from the kinds of devastating famine which has repeatedly plagued nations further to the south in Africa which lack such a precious natural resource. On this level, then, who is to chose between the advantages of life and the deleterious effects the rising ground water, precipitated by the dam, has on the ancient monuments?

DIRECTOR'S MESSAGE

Egypt... a land of mystery, of friendly people, of hot desert winds and lush green valley, the Nile, majestic ancient monuments, crowded streets, intrigue, hospitality.

Above all, Egypt is her people – warm, hospitable, courageous. This exhibition, *Splendors of Ancient Egypt,* is a tribute to these enduring and endearing people who, for so many millenia, have been prominent on the stage of history.

Splendors is an enchanting look at antiquity through the masterful works and creations left behind by an extraordinary civilization. To be sure, it is history. Certainly it is art. Whatever your viewpoint, you are sure to come away with respect, even awe, for the genius and creativity of these ancient people.

Hopefully, too, through this exhibition, Americans will come to know and love Egypt and her people as we have, and that through this sharing we can build a better future for all of us.

James E. Broughton
Executive Director

The exhibition *Splendors of Ancient Egypt from the Egyptian Museum, Cairo,* for which this book serves as the catalogue, is a special exhibition in many ways. On one level it represents the fruits of a productive collaboration between many individuals in the Supreme Council of Antiquities (SCA), that Egyptian government body charged with the care, preservation, and documentation of ancient Egypt's magnificent cultural past. Dr. Mohamed Saleh, Director of the Egyptian Museum, Cairo, has worked with us along every step of this involved process in order to insure that the objects requested met the most stringent of requirements established by the Egyptian government for such loans, while simultaneously exhibiting the highest aesthetic value which a discriminating, sophisticated American audience has become accustomed to demand from such shows. The curators of the Egyptian Museum were unflagging in their assistance, from granting us unrestricted access to the documentation for the objects to working long hours in the heat of July as we opened cases for photography for the catalogue. Other members of the staff also expedited the process, as did members of the security and tourist police. The directors of the sites of Giza and Luxor assisted with our visits and offered us every courtesy. Dr. Abdel Halim Nour el-Din, chair of the SCA, with whom the final negotiations were concluded, ought to be proud of the professionalism of the men and women in his department with whom we worked.

We must emphasize that there were rigorous criteria which first had to be satisfied before this particular loan could be approved. Whereas space does not permit the luxury of detailing those criteria, or the discussions which they generated, we must, nevertheless, acknowledge the enlightenment of Mr. Ibrahim Nawawy and of Dr. Nawar, acting on behalf of His Excellency Farouk Hosni, the Minister of Culture of the Arab Republic of Egypt, for accommodating their political and financial demands to the imperatives of the Florida International Museum's exhibition program and philosophy.

Because art and politics are one, all cultured individuals agree that beautiful works of art are eloquent, silent ambassadors capable of building bridges of understanding and tolerance between countries and cultures. On this plain, then, *Splendors of Ancient Egypt* will serve as a constant reminder of the progressive forces within the Arab Republic of Egypt. The men and women in Egypt who have been and continue to be so disposed in their outlook have not only made this exhibition possible, but continue, on yet another level, to support and foster the Middle East peace process.

It is the desire, therefore, of the Florida International Museum that this exhibition will remind its visitors of the crucial role Egypt has played, and continues to play, not only in the history of world art but also in the history of the world itself.

Robert Steven Bianchi
Exhibition Curator

ACKNOWLEDGEMENTS

**Florida International Museum
Founding Underwriters**
City of St. Petersburg
Florida Progress Corporation
The St. Petersburg Times
John and Rosemary Galbraith

**Splendors of Ancient Egypt
Exhibition Sponsors**
Barnett Bank of Pinellas County
Bayfront Life Services Inc.
Busch Gardens, Tampa Bay
EgyptAir
Eller Media Co.
Publix Super Markets, Inc.
Raymond James Financial
Southtrust Bank
Stouffer Renaissance Vinoy Resort
University of South Florida
WFLA-TV

**Florida International Museum
Directors**
Mr. John Wm. Galbraith,
Chairman
Mr. John H. O'Hearn,
Vice Chairman
Mr. Joseph F. Cronin,
President and C.E.O.
Mr. Martin J. Normile,
Secretary
Mr. W. Richard Johnston,
Treasurer
Mr. Dale W. Cassidy
Dr. Jack B. Critchfield
Mr. Ira Mitlin
Mr. L. Eugene Oliver, Jr.
Mrs. Sharon E. Simms

Ex-Officio
Honorable David J. Fischer
Honorable Connie Kone
Mr. Herbert E. Polson

**Exhibition Development
and Production by
Broughton International Inc.**

Executive Staff
James E. Broughton,
Executive Director
Dr. Robert S. Bianchi, *Curator*
Robert Tamboli, *Director of
Finance and Administration*
Mark Broughton,
Director of Operations
Stephanie Kramer,
Director of Public Relations
Margaret Bowman,
Director of Volunteers
James E. Broughton, Jr.,
Director of Merchandising
Clementine Brown,
Director of Sales and Marketing
Tracey Ballard, *Director of Group
Sales and Ticket Administration*
Mark Maksimowicz,
Director of Security
Malcolm H. Leslie, C.E.C.,
Director of Food Service

Exhibition Design
Harvard Jolly Clees Toppe
  Architects, PA, AID
Jonathan R. Toppe, AIA,
Principal Designer
Merrill David Wright,
Project Manager

Exhibition Construction
Irwin Construction Company
Innes Irwin, *President*
Rob Parker, *Project Manager*

Volunteer Administration
Margaret Bowman, *Director*
Ann Yagle, *Assistant to Director*
Jim Meyers, *Assistant*

Education
Dr. Robert S. Bianchi, *Curator*
University of South Florida,
 St. Petersburg Campus
William Heller, *Dean*

Merchandising
James E. Broughton, Jr., *Director*
Kathy Mabe, *Manager*
Kelly Tamman, *Assistant Manager*
Mindi Miles, *Administrative
Assistant*
Brooke Delucia, *Inventory Control*
Zachary Bennett, *Inventory Control*
Rifaat Hassan, *Consultant*

**Public Relations, Advertising,
and Special Events**
Stephanie Kramer, *Director*
Shara Lawson, *Coordinator
of Public Relations Services*
Chameleon Studio
Tucker Hall, Inc.
Winner Koenig & Associates
Event Makers Corporation
Wizard's Works

Operations
Mark Broughton, *Director*

Orientation Film
Media Works Inc.
Glenn Martin
Phil Schwartz

Audio Guide
Antennae
Chris Tellis
Kathy Baldwin

Catalogue
Booth-Clibborn Editions
Edward Booth-Clibborn, *Publisher*

Mark Sutcliffe, *Editor*
Phil Sayer, *Photographer*
David Hillman, *Art Director,
Pentagram Design*

Building Maintenance
Mitlin Properties Inc.
Ira Mitlin, *President*
Eileen Webber, *Property Manager*
Lisa Ulrich, *Assistant
Property Manager*
Eloise Walsh, *Coordinator,
Property Management*

Sales and Marketing
Clementine Brown, *Director*
Andree Couture, *Marketing
Representative*
Linda Dyer, *Marketing
Representative*
Sirpa Anderson, *Marketing
Assistant*

**Group Events and
Ticket Administration**
Tracey Ballard, *Director*
Linda Urtnowski, *Assistant*

Finance and Administration
Robert Tamboli, *Director*
Karen Hughes Gras,
Administrative Coordinator
Fay Beth Broughton,
Administrative Assistant
Rick Coffey, *Supervisor,
Cash Control*
Delores Remp, *Cash Control*
Stacey Lasley, *Cash Control*
Gail Hollis, *Receptionist*
Maggie Clemens, *Mail Clerk*
Matthew Wright, *Accountant*

Food Service
Malcolm H. Leslie, *C.E.C., Director*

Security
Mark Maksimowicz, *Director*

Previous page
**A view of the Pyramids at Sakkara
showing the Giza Pyramids
in the distance**
Sakkara, lying some 15 miles south
of the Giza plateau, became the burial
place of the royalty and nobility
during the Old Kingdom, while
Memphis was the capital; it is perhaps
best known for the funerary complex
of Djoser (pages 40-41). Although
superseded by the Theban necropolis
during the New Kingdom, Sakkara
continued to be used by the elite over
almost 3000 years, as tombs dating
to the Ptolemaic Period reveal.
In 1850 Auguste Mariette, the French
archaeologist, discovered the famous
Serapeum at Sakkara, where the
sacred Apis Bulls were buried in huge
sarcophagi within vast subterranean
chambers.

Map of Egypt
The Arab Republic of Egypt covers an
area of 387,000 square miles – about
equal to the size of Texas – of which
96.4 percent is desert. Its population
of over 60 million is twice that of the
next most populous Arab country
(Morocco) and makes a quarter of
the total population of the Arab
world. Around 65 percent of
Egyptians work on the land. The land
itself is a freak of nature, whose
lifeblood is the River Nile. From the
Sudanese border in the south to the
shores of the Mediterranean in the
north, the Nile Valley and its Delta
are flanked by arid desert. Egypt has
been called the gift of the Nile, for
without the river it could not exist as
a fertile, populous country, let alone
have nurtured a great civilization
some five thousand years ago. This
map shows the principal
archaeological sites, as well as other
sites of interest mentioned in the text.
A smaller map of the various sites at
Thebes is found on page 120.

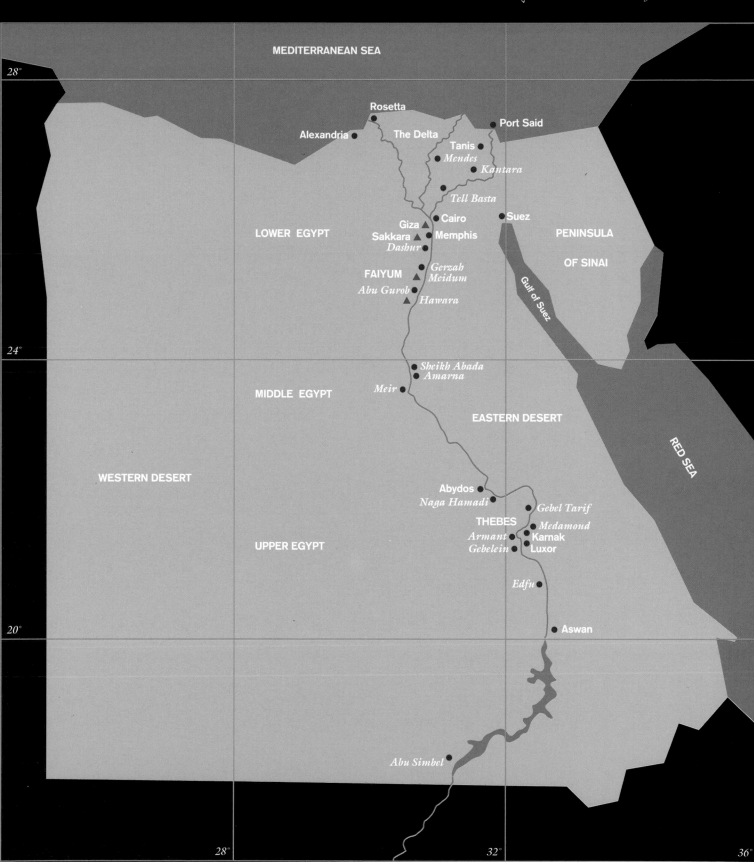

MEDITERRANEAN SEA

28°

Rosetta

Alexandria ● Port Said ●

The Delta

Tanis ●

Mendes

Kantara

Tell Basta

Cairo ● Suez ●

LOWER EGYPT Giza ▲

Sakkara ▲ Memphis ●

Dashur ●

FAIYUM ▲ *Gerzah*

Meidum ●

Abu Gurob ▲

Hawara

PENINSULA

OF SINAI

Gulf of Suez

24°

Sheikh Abada ●

Amarna ●

MIDDLE EGYPT

Meir ●

EASTERN DESERT

RED SEA

WESTERN DESERT

Abydos ●

Naga Hamadi ●

Gebel Tarif ●

THEBES *Medamoud*

Armant ● Karnak ●

UPPER EGYPT *Gebelein* ● Luxor

Edfu

20° Aswan ●

Abu Simbel ●

28° 32° 36°

INTRODUCTION

Interest in ancient Egypt as a land of enchantment and wonder never seems to wane. With the passing of each year, new discoveries in the Nile Valley charge our imaginations with excitement. Is the Great Sphinx on the Giza Plateau really older than the Great Pyramids? Will archaeologists discover a treasure more opulent than Tutankhamun's when they penetrate the burial chamber of the recently re-entered royal tomb in the Valley of the Kings? These energizing events and the profusion of ancient Egyptian themes on television and in the print media envelop all of us in a cloud of enthusiasm about ancient Egypt. Often, however, that cloud prevents us from looking more critically at ancient Egypt's cultural landscape. As a result our preconceived notions about that glorious ancient culture are wrapped in the mist of what I should like to term "the symbolists." Allow me to explain.

The monumental stone temples of ancient Egypt and the tombs of the nobles with their vividly painted scenes were crafted for the benefit of an elite which at no time numbered more than approximately 10% of the ancient Egyptian population. The members of this elite were ultra-conservative and doggedly traditional. It is for this reason that many visitors to collections of ancient Egyptian art often exclaim, "it all looks the same!" (pages 212-213). This apparent similarity may be profitably ascribed to the cultural characteristics just mentioned, but it may equally be attributed to the elite's insistence upon guarding its advantaged station in life. Its members rarely, if ever, shared their power with others, and that power was vested in knowledge, a knowledge of the hieroglyphs, from the ancient Greek words meaning, "sacred writing." By means of these pictures the ancient Egyptian elite developed a visual vocabulary which accentuated the position of pharaoh and enabled its learned scribes to speculate about life, death, and resurrection. It afforded the elite the means to detail their religious and cultural beliefs. No one except a member of the elite was taught how to read and write the hieroglyphs, a system which took approximately fifteen years to master. The very nature of the complexity of this form of writing prevented strangers from prying into their meanings.

When the inquisitive Greeks began to visit Egypt in increasingly large numbers in the seventh century B.C., first as mercenaries and later as tourists, they hounded members of the ancient Egyptian elite for information about ancient Egyptian hieroglyphs. Several centuries later the Romans did the same. Unswerving in their resolve, the members of the Egyptian elite refused to divulge information about their language to strangers. Time and again the ancient Egyptian texts caution one against revealing the secrets of the hiero-glyphs to outsiders, as the following reveals: *This is a papyrus-scroll for under-standing the words of the scriptoria... they are to be used... without the knowledge of the man-in-the-street...* Other texts contain this admonition as well: *Do not reveal this wisdom to others!* Wisdom, or knowledge was, however, passed on, but only from father to son, because of the hereditary nature of the elite. Ancient Egyptian texts repeatedly stress this point in no uncertain terms. The owner of a stela, or inscribed stone, now in the Louvre in Paris, declares: *Knowledge was not revealed to anyone except to me alone and the gods commanded that I pass that knowledge on, but only to my son and heir.* As a result, the Greeks and Romans concocted the false impression that the Egyptians, as scribes, were enrolled in secret societies whose members encoded arcane information in hieroglyphs which had to be interpreted rather than read. These same Greeks and Romans also claimed that all of this vital information was stored in vast scriptoria, or temple libraries. In point of fact these ancient Egyptian prohibitions against revealing the secrets of the hieroglyphs to strangers are nothing more than a caution against teaching those who were not members of the elite how to read and write the hieroglyphs. Accompanying the fall of ancient Egyptian civilization was the loss of the ability to read the hieroglyphs. Subsequent scholars in the West, who could read Greek and Latin, based their observations of the ancient Egyptian hieroglyphs on those Classical texts. Such scholars continued to perpetuate the false impression that the hieroglyphs were similar to a modern micro dot, that is, that each sign had to be interpreted in order to reveal its wisdom. These same individuals also claimed that the destruction of the scriptoria was intentional in order to prevent others from gaining an insight into this elevated wisdom of the putative ancient Egyptian sages.

The study of ancient Egyptian civilization along these lines accelerated during the Middle Ages and continued to mushroom through the eighteenth century. During these long centuries the research accumulated and taught was based on what the Greek and Latin authors had to say about ancient Egypt. So strong was this symbolist approach to ancient Egypt that scholars refused to entertain the suggestion that the hieroglyphs might be a language subject to the same rules of grammar and syntax as any other language. So dominant was this symbolist approach that initial attempts by Jean François Champollion were in vain because he himself had been persuaded of its correctness. Then, with the aid of the Rosetta Stone, Champollion abandoned the symbolist approach and in 1822 announced his decipherment of the hieroglyphs. He demonstrated that the hieroglyphs were a language which followed very clear rules of grammar and syntax. The symbolists were outraged by his announcement because the translations of the hieroglyphs proposed by Champollion and other scholars after him did not contain the kinds of arcane information which the Greek and Latin texts claimed were contained within them. Schooled in the principles developed first by Champollion and a host of scholars after him, the secrets of the hieroglyphs are revealed because scholars can now read the texts. The symbolists, however, continue to refuse to accept that the ancient Egyptian admonitions against sharing the secrets of the hieroglyphs are basically just cautions against teaching strangers how to read them. By learning how to read these hieroglyphs, their "secrets," or contents, would be revealed, and the advantaged stations in life enjoyed by the members of the elite would be compromised and challenged.

During the course of the nineteenth century the symbolist approach to ancient Egyptian culture continued even after the proven decipherment of the hieroglyphs by Champollion. The American author, Herman Melville, employs the symbolist tradition in his great novel *Moby Dick*. The great white whale is his work's hieroglyph which needs to be interpreted as the plot develops. So tied is this work to the symbolist approach that Melville's description of Queequeg's tattoo is virtually a verbal picture of the famous zodiac from the Temple of Hathor at Dendera which the French removed and exhibited in the Louvre in Paris. The hubbub about the curse of Tutankhamun following the discovery of his tomb in 1922 by Howard Carter is part and parcel of this same symbolist tradition, rooted in an imperfect understanding of ancient Egyptian culture as erroneously presented by certain Greek and Roman authors, and uncritically espoused by subsequent individuals.

As a result, the debate between the symbolists and the Egyptologists continues to this day. One can best regard this debate as two parallel, but non-intersecting, avenues of investigation. Consequently, some of the symbolists maintain that the Great Sphinx at Giza is older than the Pyramids around it. These individuals can quote almost one thousand years worth of references to support their positions, because the symbolist tradition is at least that old. Egyptologists,

The conservative nature of the Egyptian elite, and their exclusive knowledge of the hieroglyphs, ensured their survival and explains the apparent lack of progression in their art over a period of more than two thousand years.

on the other hand, who can both translate the hieroglyphs and render their true meanings, are at odds with this approach, and understandably so.

The exhibition for which this catalogue was written attempts to present ancient Egypt to a North American audience through the eyes of the ancient Egyptians themselves. The cloud of enthusiasm has been purposefully blown away so that the bright sunlight can illuminate the ancient land of the Nile, allowing the visitor to understand the ancient Egyptians and appreciate their cultural achievements in their own right without the intermediaries of foreign interpreters.

That understanding and appreciation can only occur when one understands the fundamental role the hieroglyphs play in ancient Egyptian culture. These signs, which numbered approximately 700 during the Middle Kingdom (about 2000 B.C.) and increased tenfold by the time of the Ptolemaic Period some 1700 years later, are basically abstractions of actual objects found in the real world of the ancient Egyptian environment. And yet, as is almost self-evident, there are many more abstract concepts in the minds of men and women than there are objects in the real world. And so it was that the ancient Egyptians had to press these pictures of real things into service in order to express abstract concepts. The task was a daunting one. Nevertheless, the ancient Egyptians did manage to express in very eloquent terms indeed their beliefs in the mechanisms of resurrection in the hereafter, and they poignantly articulated their adherence to an ethical social code which specified that they care for the less fortunate. Ancient Egypt was, and remains, a land of enchantment and wonder. It is hoped that this exhibition will reveal the true nature of this fantastic culture.

One of the objectives of this exhibition is to present Egyptian civilization in its broadest terms. As a result, discussions of the minutiae of historical events and the endless succession of pharaohs and dynasties have been kept to a minimum. In their place one will read about mathematics, medicine, literature, societal values, and the relationships between art and hieroglyphs.

I have to say a word or two about dates and names. In general, the ancient Egyptians themselves appear to have divided their history into dynasties grouped into kingdoms. Such chronologies, termed "Kings' Lists" by convention, were often inscribed on the walls of temples. It appears that such documents were the source for later compilations of the kind drafted by Manetho, an Egyptian priest of the third century B.C., who was asked to write a history of his country in Greek for the benefit of Ptolemy II Philadelphos, the then Macedonian Greek pharaoh of Egypt. Although Manetho's work has not survived, passages from it were quoted by later Greek and Latin authors. A careful study of such documents in conjunction with the preserved inscriptions enables scholars to present the history of ancient Egypt in broad strokes. However, all specialists are in agreement that it is extremely difficult, if not impossible, to establish an exact date for specific events in Egypt before Dynasty 26 which begins in 656 B.C. As a result of this recognized imprecision, I have adopted the practice of rounding off the dates of dynasties and reigns in the hope that such approximations will make it easier for a museum visitor to calculate the time differences between the objects on view and our own time. For ease of reference, therefore, we have included a chronological table on pages 26-27 which utilizes these approximate dates, and have preceded it with a Time Line on pages 24-25 along which selected objects on view in the exhibition have been reproduced in their chronological sequence. The Map on page 17 contains the locations of the known find-spots of the objects in the exhibition.

Equally problematic for a museum audience is the lack of uniformity in the spellings of ancient Egyptian proper names. Some of this is due to the nature of

The trilingual inscription on the Rosetta Stone – in Greek, Egyptian hieroglyphs, and Demotic – enabled Champollion to announce his decipherment of the Egyptian scripts in 1822. The symbolists refused to accept Champollion's breakthrough.

the evidence which compels some scholars to use an arbitrary transliteration of the hieroglyphs, that is assigning the hieroglyphs specific letters of our alphabet. Other scholars prefer to render these same names in accordance with the spellings as found in either Greek or Latin texts. Since there is really no way out of this confusion, we have opted for a system which employs the spellings of ancient Egyptian names in their more commonly encountered forms. In an attempt to maintain internal consistency, the same spellings of elements which appear in several different proper names remain consistent, and that internal consistency, it is hoped, will enable the visitor to detect that similarity, and to recognize their relationships. So, for example, Amun, a god's name, is spelled the same when it appears as an element in the pharaoh Tutankhamun's name. In like manner, the masculine name Nefer is retained in Neferet, its feminine form. When the choice exists, we have selected the form representing a transliteration of the Egyptian hieroglyphs, for example, Senuseret, rather than the Greek version, Sesostris.

The dimension of each object is given as the greatest measurement in height, width, or diameter. That dimension is always given in inches because of the reluctance of the American public to embrace the metric system.

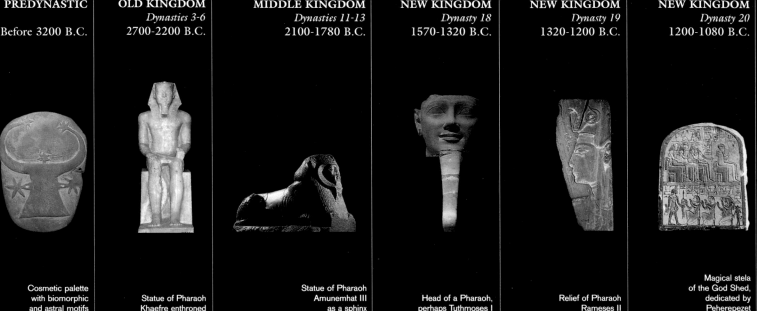

PREDYNASTIC	OLD KINGDOM	MIDDLE KINGDOM	NEW KINGDOM	NEW KINGDOM	NEW KINGDOM
Before 3200 B.C.	*Dynasties 3-6* 2700-2200 B.C.	*Dynasties 11-13* 2100-1780 B.C.	*Dynasty 18* 1570-1320 B.C.	*Dynasty 19* 1320-1200 B.C.	*Dynasty 20* 1200-1080 B.C.

Cosmetic palette with biomorphic and astral motifs

Statue of Pharaoh Khaefre enthroned

Statue of Pharaoh Amunemhat III as a sphinx

Head of a Pharaoh, perhaps Tuthmoses I

Relief of Pharaoh Rameses II

Magical stela of the God Shed, dedicated by Peherepezet

LATE PERIOD
Dynasties 26-31
656-332 B.C.

PTOLEMAIC
PERIOD
332-30 B.C.

ROMAN
IMPERIAL
PERIOD
30 B.C.-330 A.D.

Statue of the God
Osiris enthroned

Stela of the
Macedonian Greek
Pharaoh Ptolemy V
Epiphanes offering to
the sacred Buchis Bull

Statue of an
enthroned official

DATE	PHARAOH	EGYPT	REST OF THE WORLD
PREDYNASTIC PERIOD Before 3200 B.C.		Changes in ecological system in northeast Africa; pottery, stone vessels and palettes; more developed forms of mudbrick architecture; elite tombs	First urban civilization in the world in Sumer, Southern Mesopotamia
ARCHAIC PERIOD Dynasties 1-2 3200-2700 B.C.	*Kaa*	Hieroglyphs appear in their fully developed form. Unification of the Two Lands; foundation of Memphis; Step Pyramid of Djoser at Sakkara	Cuneiform script in Mesopotamia Silk weaving in China
OLD KINGDOM Dynasties 3-6 2700-2200 B.C. Dynasty 4	*Kufu, Khaefre, Menkaure*	Period of absolute monarchs; Great Pyramids and Sphinz at Giza	
Dynasties 5-6	*Unas, Pipi I, Pipi II*	Pyramids at Sakkara; Pyramid Texts; elite begins to rival authority and status of pharaoh; trade with Lebanon, Aegean Islands, Syria, Africa	European Bronze Age
FIRST INTERMEDIATE PERIOD Dynasties 7-11 2200-2050 B.C.	*Merekare, Neferkare*	Egypt politically fragmented into warring, local elite groups	
MIDDLE KINGDOM Dynasties 11-13 2100-1780 B.C.	*Amunemhat III, Montuhotep Nebhepetere, Senuseret I, II*	Pyramid at Hawara; Faiyum developed for its agricultural potential; statues of elite marked with signs of age for first time; Classical Period for hieroglyphs and literature	Stonehenge Formation of states on Minoan Crete
SECOND INTERMEDIATE PERIOD Dynasties 14-17 1780-1570 B.C.	*Apophis, Ramose, Ahmoses, Ahmosesnefertari, Sekenere Taaken*	Egypt occupied by foreigners: Hyksos in the Delta, Kushites/Nubians in the south around Aswan. Local elite vie for supremacy; Theban elite emerges victorious	
NEW KINGDOM Dynasty 18 1570-1320 B.C.	*Hatshepsut, Tuthmoses III, Amunhotep III, Akhenaton, Horemheb,*	Empire Period; Thebes capital; royal tombs in Valley of the Kings, Valley of the Queens; Karnak and Luxor temples enlarged; Amarna founded and abandoned.	Mycenean period First written inscriptions in China
Dynasty 19 1320-1200 B.C.	*Tutankhamun, Sety I, Rameses II, Merenptah*	Wars against the Hittites; world's first mutual Non-Agression Pact; monumental architecture at Abu Simbel; Rameseum; first mention of Israel in Egyptian documents	
Dynasty 20 1200-1080 B.C.	*Rameses III, RamesesVI*	Sea peoples; Harem Conspiracy; Egypt's security threatened; Medinet Habu	Collapse of Hittite Empire
THIRD INTERMEDIATE PERIOD Dynasties 21-25 1080-656 B.C.			
Dynasty 21	*Psusennes I, Amunemopet*	Pharaohs rule from Tanis; counter-kings at Thebes; period of unsurpassed accomplishments in mummification and metallurgy; royal tombs at Tanis	Emergence of kingdom of Israel

DATE	PHARAOH/RULER	EGYPT	REST OF THE WORLD
Dynasty 22	*Sheshonk II*	Pharaohs continue to be buried in royal tombs at Tanis; threats from Kushites and abroad	Foundation of powerful Assyrian empire
Dynasties 23-25	*Piankhy, Shabako, Taharka*	Warring local elites; invasion of the Kushites (beginning of Dynasty 25); Divine Wives of Amun; order restored; Assyrian invasions; petty princes of the Delta city of Sais emerge as a political force	First Greek alphabetic inscription
LATE PERIOD Dynasties 26-31 656-332 B.C.			
Dynasty 26	*Psamtik I, Psamtik II, Amasis, Apries*	The Saite Renaissance, capital at Sais; Palace at Memphis; private tombs at Sakkara; interaction with emerging Greek city states.	Beginning of Archaic period in Greece; foundation of vast Achaemenid empire of Persia, stretching from Egypt to the Indus
Dynasty 27 525-404 B.C.	*Cambyses, Darius the Great*	Persians invade and make Egypt a satrapy – a province of their empire; elite conspires with Persians; tombs at Sakkara	Classical period in Greece; completion of Parthenon
Dynasties 28-29		Ephemeral dynasties; warring local elites	
Dynasty 30		Last native Egyptians to rule the country until Abd al-Nasser in 1956	
Dynasty 31	*Artaxerxes III*	Persians reconquer Egypt	Alexander the Great conquers Egypt and Persia and reaches India. Hellenism established in Asia
PTOLEMAIC PERIOD 332-30 B.C.	*Ptolemy, son of Lagos Ptolemy II Philadelphos Ptolemy V Epiphanes Cleopatra the Great*	Egypt falls into the hands of Alexander the Great without a battle; Ptolemy founds a Macedonian Greek dynasty; foundation of Alexandria with its Pharos, Library, Museum, Tomb of Alexander the Great	Romans destroy Greek states, though Greek culture still predominant. Parthians take control of Persia, Mesopotamia and parts of Central Asia
ROMAN IMPERIAL PERIOD 30 B.C.-330 A.D.	*Augustus, Tiberius, Nero, Domitian, Trajan, Hadrian, Septimus Severus, Caracalla,*	Octavian, later Augustus, conquers Egypt; Egyptian elite collaborates with Roman emperors	
60	*Constantine the Great, Decius, Diocletian*	Tradition maintains St. Mark brings Christianity to Egypt	Rome largest city in world (population 1 million)
313		Edict of Milan guarantees freedom of religious practices throughout the Roman Empire	Sassanians defeat Parthians, foundation of Sassanian empire
			Constantine founds new eastern capital of Roman Empire at Constantinople
CHRISTIAN/ BYZANTINE PERIOD 330-641			
330		Partition of Roman Empire into east and west; Egypt falls under eastern, or Byzantine, sphere	
451		Council of Chalcedon leads to formation of an Independent Coptic (Egyptian Christian) Church with its own patriarch, or spiritual authority, and a strict adherence to its Monophysite doctrine	Cathedral of St. Sophia, Constantinople built by Justinian
ISLAMIC PERIOD 641 to the present			Hegira of Mohammed; beginning of Muslim era; Umayyad Caliphate comes to power. Islamic empire covers one third of the Old World
641		Arab conquest of Egypt; introduction of Islam	

THE PREDYNASTIC PERIOD

In our modern high tech world with its information highway, microwave ovens and satellite dish televisions, it is easy to lose sight of the earlier inventions which fundamentally changed the course of human history. One such invention was farming; another was writing. It is to the development of these two technological innovations in the Nile Valley that one now turns, because ancient Egypt was essentially an agricultural society which was ruled by those who had a command of the language. The histories of the emergence of agriculture and the development of language can be linked to the emergence of the Egyptian elite. And that elite, firmly established at the dawn of Egyptian history, created the institutions–administrative, religious, and cultural – which the elite perpetuated virtually unchanged for the next four millennia.

Herodotus, the father of history, wrote in about 450 B.C., "Egypt is the gift of the River Nile." In order to assess the importance of that statement one needs a brief geography lesson. Egypt is situated in the northeastern quadrant of the African continent, and represents the last leg of the Nile River's long march to the Mediterranean Sea. That march begins almost three thousand miles to the south of the modern city of Alexandria. Here in the heart of Central Africa the waters of Lake Victoria form the White Nile, which flows for a distance of some 1,500 miles to Khartoum, the capital of the modern nation state of the Sudan. Here at Khartoum the White Nile is joined by the Blue Nile, a river which begins 1,000 miles to the south of that same city in far-off Lake Tana in the modern nation state of Ethiopia. The confluence of the White and Blue Niles at Khartoum marks the beginning of the River Nile proper, whose course to the Mediterranean Sea is almost 2,000 miles long. The rains which fall each spring in Central Africa combine with the melting snows on the Ethiopian highlands and contribute to the run-off which swells the waters of the Blue Nile. This run-off collects a quantity of rich red earth which rushes forth causing its flood waters to reach Egypt in late summer. Because the Nile River flows from south to north, the southern part of Egypt lies in what is termed Upper Egypt, because one has to travel upstream in order to reach it. On the other hand, the northern part of the country is designated Lower Egypt. In antiquity, then, this annual flood would inundate the land of Egypt beginning in the south, or Upper Egypt. When it subsided, the alluvial soil left behind was very fertile and could be easily prepared for sowing. When combined both with the ready supply of water available throughout the year from the Nile itself and with the nurturing rays of the warm Egyptian sun, the alluvial soil became the foundation of Egypt's agricultural dynamism which compelled the ancients to refer to Egypt as "the bread basket of the world."

But it took time before the ancient Egyptians realized the potential of the Nile's annual inundation. By the eighth millennium B.C. the inhabitants of the Nile Valley, who may very well have intermarried with peoples from neighboring regions (pages 148-151), developed a society characterized as one of "hunter-gatherers." They possessed the ability to craft stone into grinders for the processing of plants which formed an important part of their diet.

Certain natural changes in the ecological systems of northeastern Africa during the course of the sixth millennium B.C. accelerated the transformation of the hunter-gatherer society into a more sedentary one with an emphasis on both animal husbandry and agriculture. The peoples farther to the south of Africa as well as those in Mesopotamia, that is the land between the Tigris and Euphrates rivers, both had an impact on this transformation. It has been convincingly suggested that the first plants grown by these early Egyptian farmers were those cultivated earlier in the south, as the presence of melon, the seeds for which were used both for nourishing soups and pharmaceuticals, suggests.

These early Egyptians lived in settled communities as attested by the fragmentary remains of huts which have been excavated and studied by Egyptologists. They seem to have been accomplished farmers as seen in the traces of storage pits, lined with reed mats, which served as early forms of grain silos. Communal hearths have also been uncovered in which faunal experts have identified the charred bones of animals such as the crocodile and antelope as well as those of cattle, pig, sheep, and goat. A few tantalizing scraps of spun and woven linen, recovered from such early sites as well, suggest that flax, from which linen is made, was also being cultivated. The Egyptians were beginning to wear hand-made clothing.

Life in these early villages can be suggested by the meticulous work of Egyptologists who carefully excavated cemeteries and methodically recorded what they found in each and every grave. Over 90% of the Predynastic Period graves excavated, which can be dated to the years between 4500-3500 B.C., contained less than 35 objects. Somewhat less than 10% of the graves in these same cemeteries contained more than 35 objects. This inequality in the number of grave goods implies a degree of social stratification and indicates the initial presence of an elite which already reveals its advantaged position in Egyptian society by virtue of its more amply supplied graves.

The emergence of the elite quickens toward the end of the Predynastic Period (3500-3000 B.C.). Once again the graves, both in their size and in their contents, enable Egyptologists to suggest the following development. Certain individuals, identified as males and not females on the basis of the forensic examination of the skeletons, emerge as leaders of the elite. These male skeletons were buried in graves, perhaps better termed tombs, which were distinguished from all other contemporary graves in the same cemetery by virtue of their infinitely larger dimensions as well as by the greater number of offerings and grave goods found within them. Moreover, the tombs of these advantaged males were grouped together into their own special sections of the cemetery. They were purposefully segregated from the other contemporary interments on the site. One site contained almost 2,500 burials of which only about 60, or less than 3%, belong to the elite category just described. Clearly these men were gaining control of the existing social systems-political, religious, economic, and the like.

Egyptologists have suggested that the emergence of this elite occurred at the same time as the emergence of craft specializations and an administrative bureaucracy created to oversee those activities. In addition to the obvious need for seeds for sowing, agriculture demanded the procurement of the materials and their fashioning into the implements to be used in farming-hoes, mattocks, plows, and the like. After each yearly flood, the fields had to be surveyed to establish boundaries between one farmer's land and another's. The fields themselves had to be prepared and the seed sown. The crops had to be tended until they matured. They then had to be harvested and transported either to storage areas or to processing centers. Prior to such activities the procurement of the materials necessary to construct the means of transport or to erect the storage and/or processing centers had to be insured. Finally, the intricate system of barter, by which the goods were exchanged for other goods – the ancient Egyptians did not use money in the form of coins until very late in their history – had to be monitored. This picture becomes even more complex if draught animals with their trappings become part of the process. The mind then boggles at the organization required when, in late Predynastic times, boats became

The Nile's annual inundation left a rich, thin deposit of alluvial soil, creating conditions whereby Egypt became known as the "bread basket of the world." Wheat, introduced from abroad, derived from that first cultivated in Mesopotamia.

necessary for the transport of those commodities. Such interlocking agricultural specializations represent but one component of a more complex system of ever expanding and ever more complicated cultural interdependencies.

It has been suggested, therefore, that certain leaders of one community did compete with leaders of adjacent communities in order to expand their respective spheres of influence. This expansion was motivated by economic, rather than military, factors so that such activities can often be regarded as strictly regulated trade agreements.

With the passing of time, leaders of one after another of these emerging villages lost their independence as their domains were successively incorporated into increasingly larger and larger geographic units each ruled by progressively more powerful members. In the end, around 3000 B.C., virtually all of these units in Upper Egypt were united under one monarch, whose successors eventually incorporated Lower Egypt into their realm.

The details of this process of the "Unification of the Two Lands," as Upper and Lower Egypt were anciently termed, and the identification of the principal figures involved are imprecisely known. This imprecision raises a very interesting point regarding the ancient Egyptians and their own history. A visitor may find it extraordinary that the ancient Egyptians did not seem to focus on what we today might call milestone events and personalities. Whereas we moderns seem to enjoy celebrating the birthday of George Washington, the father of our country, the ancient Egyptians do not appear to have bothered to record the name of the individual responsible for uniting the two lands for the very first time around 3000 B.C. Tradition, and the Greek and Latin historians, credit one Menes with this achievement, but Egyptologists are less certain of the identity because ancient Egyptians contemporary with the event appear to have passed it over in silence. This apparent lack of concern over crediting specific individuals with specific accomplishments contributes to a modern's imperfect knowledge of ancient Egyptian history. And yet that silence about such events is very eloquent in another, very important regard. The ancient Egyptian elite was a societal collective in which the individual as an individual played no role. The elite functioned and lasted for as long as it did because each and every member deferred to pharaoh. One's ego apparently had no place in such a communal society. Since this appears to have been the case, the community of the elite, as a whole, saw no need to single out any one individual for special recognition for contributing to the enhanced status of the group as a whole.

According to one anthropological model, the elite developed a rather neat public relations campaign, the aim of which successfully caused increasingly larger numbers of people to join forces voluntarily with increasingly smaller numbers of leaders. In so doing the majority of the population gave up whatever rights it may have had. How was this possible? One explanation is that the elite convinced the masses that their submissive and subjectional social roles would confer upon them greater benefits afforded by collective cooperation. Others doubtless saw such alliances as a means of reinforcing their own spheres of influence, whether those areas were familial, geographic, economic, administrative, religious, or the like. Once established, the relationship between the elite and the masses appears to have remained constant and steadfast. There are virtually no references in the ancient Egyptian records as preserved today to the kinds of populist insurrections which characterize either the French or American revolutions of the eighteenth century. The approximately 90% or so of the non-elite population were apparently content with their lot in life, or at least do not appear to have expressed their dissatisfaction in terms of civil disobedience.

With the emergence of an elite, Egypt developed a complicated system of interdependent communities, each with its own leader. As time passed, the more powerful leaders assumed control over the weaker, resulting eventually, around 3,000 B.C., in the "Unification of the Two Lands."

The hieroglyphic system helped to strengthen the position of the elite. For only the elite 10%, or some 7,500 people (fewer than 20 people per mile's length of the Nile), were literate. Through its influence on Canaanite and Proto-Siniatic — an early alphabet which after many modifications passed into western usage — the hieroglyphic system can be seen as the precursor of our own language.

The members of the elite, numbering less than 10% of the population, required a method of insuring their advantaged station in life. They were compelled to develop and establish a method of communication, known only to their members, which could be easily recognizable and might be used to identify that one member of the elite who was its undisputed leader and who is traditionally identified as pharaoh. One means of achieving this goal was to develop a system of communication to which only the elite had access.

It has been convincingly argued, therefore, that the elite enlisted the services of one of its members who conceived of the hieroglyphic system of writing. That one and only one member of the elite, and not a committee, was responsible for this invention seems assured because the hieroglyphs, as a system of writing, do not appear to have undergone a long period of development. In other words, the hieroglyphs seem to have been introduced fully developed. Here again, the name of the inventor of this remarkable means of communication was apparently not deemed worthy of recording.

An important, but often generally overlooked, aspect about ancient Egyptian hieroglyphs is that they are in fact the basis of the alphabet which we use today! The history of the development of our alphabet can be summarized as follows, and occurred in the land of Canaan.

The civilized world of the eastern end of the Mediterranean basin generally employed one of two forms of writing. One was the ancient Egyptian hieroglyphs and the second was cuneiform, from the Latin words for "wedge-shaped," because this best describes the appearance of the written language of the civilizations of ancient Mesopotamia. Then, about 1600 B.C., about a dozen or so inscriptions were composed in a script which Sir Flinders Petrie, the father of modern archaeology, called Proto-Siniatic. He had discovered these inscriptions at the site of Serabeit al-Khadim in the Sinai.

This early alphabet could have either 27 or 28 letters. As time passed more and more inscriptions in this alphabet were found in a developing form in various locations in what is now the modern nation state of Israel. This further development impelled scholars to term these inscriptions Proto-Canaanite, a term which is exclusively geographic in nature. Soon this system spread throughout the Canaanite and Phoenician lands. Although not strictly an alphabet because each sign stands for a consonant and a vowel, this Proto-Canaanite alphabet did contribute to literacy because it was soon standardized to some 22 individual signs by the time of the thirteenth century B.C. These 22 signs are far less numerous than the hundreds of hieroglyphs in use at the time. It was, then, in this form that this early form of the alphabet was transmitted to the people of the city-state of Ugarit, or Ras Shamra, on the coast of the modern nation state of Syria. They further refined the system and were the first people in the world to list these signs in a kind of a,b,c. It was this form of the alphabet which was further modified by the Greeks until it passed via the Romans into the alphabet one uses in the West today. So, in a very real sense, the English alphabet with which the words in this very catalogue are written, is actually indebted to the ancient Egyptian hieroglyphs on which it is ultimately based.

It is important to remember, however, that it was only members of the elite, that 10% of Egyptian society, who were conversant with the hieroglyphs. This book therefore deals with the artistic production of that elite and of the pharaohs who stood at their head.

**Cosmetic palette with biomorphic
and astral motifs** (left)
Predynastic period, 4000-3000 B.C.
Graywacke, 6" in height
From Gerzah; JE 43103

**Cosmetic palette in the form
of a fish** (above left)
Predynastic period, 4000-3000 B.C.
Graywacke, 5 1/2" in length
From Naga Hamadi; JE 71323

**Cosmetic palette with incised
animal motifs** (above center)
Predynastic period, 4000-3000 B.C.
Graywacke, 9 1/2" in height
From Naga Hamadi; JE 71326
Palettes such as these appear to have
been implements upon which green
malachite was ground, which was
then used as an ancient Egyptian
equivalent of mascara to line the eyes.
Such palettes were often interred with
the deceased in burials of the
Predynastic Period where, more often
than not, they were placed in the
vicinity of the head. As a result, their
function appears to have transcended
a merely cosmetic purpose.
Inscriptions from later periods reveal
that the ancient Egyptians believed
that evil might enter into the body
through the five orifices of the head,
of which the eyes were the most easily
breached access. As a result, the
green malachite appears to have been
magically used to prevent evil from
gaining such easy access.

Imitation stone vessel
Predynastic period, 4000-3000 B.C.
Painted pottery, 6 1/4" in height
Findspot not known; 2/7/18/1
One of the most remarkable aspects
of ancient Egyptian art is the ability
of its craftsmen to imitate in paint
virtually every material found in the
Egyptian landscape. That
characteristic was already in place
in the formative, Predynastic Period,
as this pottery vessel, painted in
imitation of stone, perhaps granite,
reveals. Whereas the motivation for
such imitations may have been
economic, because it appears to have
been economically less expensive to
craft a painted pottery vessel than to
carve one out of stone, the possibility
also exists that the motivation may
have been symbolic. Clay was
considered to be a primeval material
which contained essential life-bearing
forces and granite was a material often
associated with the sun gods. The
artful combination of both materials
in one vessel may have symbolically
provided its owner with enhanced
powers of resurrection.

**Red on buff vessel
with a boating scene
Predynastic Period, 3500-3000 B.C.
Painted pottery; 5" in height
Findspot not known; JE 88124**

During the course of the Predynastic Period, as the individual members of the emerging elite gained increasingly greater control over the land, the decorative scheme of the pottery changed as the white cross-line paint of the earlier phase gave way to the red paint on a buff-colored ground of the later. Again, the lack of accompanying inscriptions renders the exact identification of the motifs depicted problematic. Most scholars, however, are in accord in regarding the principal motifs on such pots as many-oared Nile vessels, the decks of which are equipped with cabins. Often these cabins have standards attached to them, which may represent either standards associated with specific deities or insignia emblematic of certain towns and their rulers.

Occasionally these pots are also decorated with figures of animals, together with an assortment of geometric and floral forms which evoke, to some scholars at least, the flora and fauna of the local landscape. Once again, the motifs are arranged in a random pattern across the surfaces of the vessel without any apparent regard for a rigorously applied organizing principle. In keeping with artistic tenets established earlier, each object is still depicted from its most characteristic vantage, because the ancient Egyptian craftsmen were interested in visual clarity and not in creating the kind of illusions of reality which have preoccupied Western artists from the time of the Renaissance.

**Two-handled stone vessels
Predynastic period; porphyry
(pages 36-37)
4 3/8" in height; from Gebel Tarif
CG 14346 (page 36)
6" in height; from Gebelein
JE 54542 (page 37)**

**Archaic period, Dynasty 1
Breccia; 5" in height
Findspot not known
CG 18627 (above)**

Stone vessels represent one of the deluxe products created by the ancient Egyptian craftsmen. The skill with which they were hollowed out, often possessing eggshell-thin walls, and the elegance of their resulting profile are often so seductively appealing to modern aesthetic sensibilities that one tends to overlook the context in which they were made. In general, all stone vessels were royal commissions, because pharaoh controlled the quarries and other sources of stone. Special expeditions were dispatched to those regions of the empire and specific religious ceremonies had to be performed before the stone could be extracted and worked into finished products. In like manner, the end of the work in those places was marked by appropriate closing prayers and rituals. Within this cultural context, then, any stone object was inherently possessed of a symbolic value which transcended its apparent function as a useful vessel.

Breccia, for example, was a stone associated in ancient Egyptian religious beliefs with guarantees of stability and inalterability. As a result, stone vessels crafted from this material would, when buried with the deceased as grave goods, magically insure the permanence of his/her aspired resurrection. In this light, it is not surprising to learn that the burial of pharaoh Djoser, owner of the Step Pyramid (pages 40-41), contained almost 40,000 stone vessels in a wide variety of material. These were doubtless prized for their amuletic, symbolic importance which superseded their value as simple containers.

It has been suggested that craftsmen were manufacturing stone vessels long before they began making stone statues. In fact, some scholars would go so far as to argue that the techniques developed for the manufacture of those stone vessels were later appropriated for the manufacture of stone statues. Indeed, the ancient Egyptian word which a modern would translate as "craft" is in fact the hieroglyph representing a stone-vase maker's drill weighted at the top with stones. In light of the skill of these early craftsmen and the symbolic associations of the stone used in the manufacture of such vessels, it is surprising that the ancient Egyptians apparently refrained for so long from erecting the tombs in stone.

THE OLD KINGDOM

Previous page
**The Step Pyramid Complex
of Pharaoh Djoser at Sakkara**
All too often, the Pyramids on the
Giza Plateau have so commanded the
attention of scholar and tourist alike,
that the achievement represented
by the Step Pyramid at Sakkara
is overlooked. Nevertheless, the Step
Pyramid represents an important
technological breakthrough because
it is the first monumental architectural
complex in ancient Egypt to have
been erected almost entirely of stone.
In order to gauge the magnitude of
this achievement of building in stone,
consider the following. Although they
possessed the requisite technologies
for working stone because of their
long established tradition of
manufacturing stone vessels (pages
36-38), the ancient Egyptians, it
sems, did not initially understand the
structural properties inherent in stone
as a building material; up to this
time they relied almost exclusively
upon mudbrick for their architectural
programs (pages 28-29). When
Djoser, as head of the elite and
director of all the craftsmen in
his realm, decided to erect his tomb
in stone, his only frame of reference
was mudbrick construction. As a
result, the quarrymen and
stonemasons literally cut larger blocks
of stone into the dimensions of the
mudbricks with which the Egyptians
were accustomed to build. Just think
of the time, energy, and cost involved
in turning blocks of stone into brick-
shaped pieces! These stone bricks
were then set into place in order to
erect Djoser's tomb, the original plan
of which was to be a mastaba of
unprecedented size. At some point in
the actual building of the tomb,
Djoser decided to alter its shape and
height by adding six additional tiers,
each made of stone. The resulting
structure, traditionally termed the
Step Pyramid, rose to an original
height of almost 200 feet, so that it
dominated the landscape (pages 188-
189). The pyramid was surrounded
by an enclosure wall about 1,700 feet
long and 900 feet wide within which
were situated not only the pyramid
itself but an array of subsidiary
buildings and altars designed to serve
the needs of Djoser's cult. More
extraordinary still is the speed with
which the technology for building in
stone developed in ancient Egypt.
In less than a century – the interval
of time separating the reign of Djoser
from that of Kufu – the Egyptians
went from building pyramids out of
tiny, brick-shaped stones to employing
blocks of stone weighing as much
as 15 tons.

With the introduction of hieroglyphs, history in Egypt begins. From the data contained within those inscriptions and the compilations of later generations of ancient Egyptians, it is possible to sketch the development of ancient Egyptian civilization during Dynasties 1 and 2, a period which is traditionally termed the Archaic Period. One of the crucial developments during this time was the establishment of a capital city at Memphis, not too far from the modern city of Cairo, at a point in the landscape where tradition maintains that Upper and Lower Egypt met. The ancient name of this city, which is today known as Memphis, was pronounced something on the order of Ineb-hedge which means "The White Wall." As with so many other issues in ancient Egyptian culture there are usually two explanations for every phenomenon, one literal and the other metaphorical. In the case of Ineb-hedge, its name may have derived from the color of the white limestone from which its architecture was erected. On another level, the name may have been intentionally selected to emphasize the domination of Upper Egypt, whose heraldic color was white, over Lower Egypt, whose heraldic color was red, since one assumes that the unification of Egypt was effected by the triumph of the Upper Egyptian elite over that of Lower Egypt. Memphis, once established, never lost its importance and continued to be a significant religious and political center throughout the entire history of Egypt right down to the Christian Period.

Oddly enough, the building material of choice during the Archaic Period remained mudbrick (pages 28-29), although stone was employed for a variety of other crafts including the manufacture of vessels (pages 36-38), palettes (page 34), and statues. One of the most perplexing, but nevertheless dominant, features of ancient Egyptian civilization is the sudden appearance of visual forms in a fully developed state without any apparent preliminary stages of development. The appearance of the hieroglyphs, already mentioned, is one such manifestation of this phenomenon. A second is the sudden, and quite unexpected, appearance of monumental stone architecture in the form of the Step Pyramid Complex of Pharaoh Netjerekhet of Dynasty 3 (pages 40-41), whom the ancient Egyptians of the Ptolemaic Period called Djoser. It is one of those quirks of fate that Djoser's reputation has been eclipsed by that of one of his officials, Imhotep by name, whose reputation is due more to the embellishments of later generations (pages 198-199), particularly by Greek and Roman authors, than to his own Egyptian contemporaries.

Manetho, an Egyptian priest asked by Ptolemy II Philadelphos, a Macedonian Greek king of Egypt, to write a history of his country in Greek in the third century B.C., was the first to claim that Imhotep was the inventor of stone architecture in Egypt. That pronouncement came over 2,000 years after the death of Imhotep. From contemporary monuments on which Imhotep's name appears one learns that he bore titles ranking him as a very high official at the court of Djoser, that he served as an important priest of the sun at Heliopolis, and that he himself was associated with the manufacture of stone vessels and was engaged in various architectural activities, the exact nature of which is not specified. None of the latter titles can be interpreted to suggest that he was the individual responsible for the decision to build in stone. This conclusion should not come as a shock to anyone because the nature of Egyptian society was such that the elite was governed by pharaoh. In this light, the decision to execute a structure in stone was pharaoh's decision. Accordingly, Imhotep, and others at the court, merely carried out pharaoh's directive. Manetho, obviously attempting to please his Macedonian Greek sovereign, contrary to the practice of the ancient Egyptians who almost never credited anyone with the invention of anything, as we have seen in the case of the inventor of the hieroglyphs. In like manner, the reputation of Imhotep was embellished by later generations which considered him to have been a physician of extraordinary talents, although the preserved inscriptions contemporary with his life contain no titles which can link him to the medical profession. There is always the danger, therefore, of accepting at face value information about ancient Egyptians written by those not contemporary with the events they are describing. Very few realize that such information is more often than not contradicted by the actual ancient Egyptian record. It is all the more regrettable in this case that more information has not survived about Djoser himself because his Step Pyramid complex at Sakkara should rank as one of the greatest wonders of ancient Egyptian architecture.

The transition from Dynasty 3 to Dynasty 4 begins with Pharaoh Seneferu, and contemporary records reveal that members of the royal family of this dynasty were deeply involved with the hands-on administration of the land of Egypt. Never before, and perhaps never afterward, has the world witnessed such absolute monarchs whose power was so great that pharaohs like Seneferu could command three pyramids, and his successor, Khnumkhuefuy, often abbreviated to Kufu, whom the Greeks called Cheops, could order the construction of the greatest of all pyramids in Egypt (pages 2-3).

From the vantage of the twentieth century, at a time when human beings have landed on the moon and traveled for extended periods of time in outer space, one stands in awe before the Great Pyramid at Giza. The modern mind boggles at the prospect of how it was constructed, and authorities constantly debate the merits of one engineering method over those of another. In the end, one supposes, a modern may never know the exact methods employed by the ancient Egyptians for building the pyramids. After all, they were notorious for not commemorating milestone events, not recording the names of their inventors, and not compiling treatises on how they went about building their monuments. But make no mistake about it—these monuments were erected by the ancient Egyptians themselves, and they had a name for each of them. So, for example, the Great Pyramid of Kufu was called "The Horizon of Kufu," whereas that of Khaefre was "Great is Khaefre." From our smug, know-it-all positions in this century, one tends to forget that technologies once introduced as part of our own industrial revolution less than two centuries ago have become so obsolete that their mechanics have been lost. How many of us can go into the woods, actually identify and collect the raw materials supplied by Nature and start a fire? How many stars in a night sky can we not see with the naked eye because of urban blight? To deny the ancient Egyptians the ability to construct these monuments and to ascribe their erection instead to other forces is to deny the human spirit of its potential.

Whereas a modern visitor might, nevertheless, still stand in awe of these architectural accomplishments, one must always recall the rather unsavory reputation these kings seem to have had in later ages. Herodotus, for example, paints a reprehensible picture of Kufu as a tyrant who forced his daughter into prostitution in order to obtain funds for his extravagant lifestyle. Despite the hyperbole of his rhetoric, there appears to be a grain of truth in his assessment of Kufu's character because a similar image of this pharaoh is presented in the Westcar Papyrus, which was acquired by the Egyptian Museum in Berlin in 1886. Several passages in that papyrus are worthy of comment.

Kufu appears suffering from ennui; he is simply bored with life and demands

Dynasties 1 and 2 (the Archaic Period) marked the foundation of Memphis as a capital city; mudbrick continued to be used for building; and the hieroglyphs first appeared in their fully developed form.

With the Old Kingdom and Dynasty 4 came pharaohs who ruled as absolute monarchs, and who left their mark on world civilization in the form of the famous pyramids at Giza.

The Great Pyramid of Kufu was known as "The Horizon of Kufu;" that of Khaefre as "Great is Khaefre."

a diversion of some sort. That diversion comes in the form of a trip on the Nile aboard his pleasure vessel. He orders a gang of female servants to man the oars, dressed in the most salacious of garments, evoking the attire of a modern burlesque queen. As they row titillating the king, one of the women loses a hair ornament in the form of a fish which falls into the Nile. She immediately stops rowing and causes a fuss. The powerful monarch, apparently unable to deal with the situation, promises the woman another hair ornament just like the one she has just lost. *I want my hair ornament, the one that fell into the river, not one just like it,* she exclaims. *Row and I'll replace it,* pleads Kufu. *But I want my hair ornament, the one that fell into the river, not one just like it,* she again screams. The king enlists the assistance of a magician who straightway causes the hair ornament to rise up to the surface on a potsherd which is immediately returned to the woman and the sailing continues. So does Kufu's ennui. He orders another diversion, this time in the form of another magician whose claim to fame is his ability to dismember animals and reassemble them, head to tail. Kufu is delighted by the prospect and asks, *is it true that you know how to join a severed head back on to its body?* To which the magician replies, *yes, I know how to reattach a head that has been severed. Splendid,* replies Kufu. *Bring me a prisoner on death row so that his execution can be effected by the severing of his head by this magician.* The magician then rebukes Kufu by stating categorically, *I don't perform that trick on people, sovereign. Indeed, it is forbidden to do that to human beings.*

However fictitious this particular account in Kufu's life may be, it nevertheless reveals that the ancient Egyptians were, by and large, possessed of a social conscience. Their concern for those less fortunate than themselves is manifest as well in their funerary beliefs (pages 162-165). If one can trust such sentiments, the members of the elite were quite progressive in their thinking because such treatises demonstrate that, in theory at least, they were concerned about the moral and ethical treatment of human beings. This observation may very well be the reason that the agricultural masses, that 90% of the population excluded from the ranks of the elite, embraced a political ideology which demanded their tacit acceptance of the submissive and subjectional social roles offered to them by that elite. The hands-on administration of the realm by members of the royal family may very well have resulted in rival claimants to the throne of Egypt following the death of Kufu. Order was finally restored under Khaefre (page 49), whose pyramid on the Giza plateau, recognizable by the remains of its cap stone at its apex, appears to be taller than that of Kufu (pages 2-3) because it is built on a rise in the landscape.

Perhaps no ancient Egyptian monument has provoked so much controversy of late as the Great Sphinx on the Giza Plateau. To traditional Egyptologists it represents the image of Khaefre (pages 18-19). As a composite beast, the Great Sphinx harmoniously combines the body of a lion with the head of the reigning monarch in such a way that the resulting figure is neither threatening nor horrifying to Western sensibilities, in the way that some Halloween monsters appear to be. This beast is a colossal version of an image introduced somewhat earlier in Dynasty 4 into the repertoire of ancient Egyptian sculpture. During the New Kingdom this colossus was venerated as a form of the god Hor of the Two Horizons by Egyptians who were doubtless aware of its Egyptian origins.

For the symbolists the Great Sphinx represents the sculptural achievements of some allegedly long-lost superior civilization which antedated that of Egypt. The proponents of such a theory support their claim with a religious zeal tantamount to that of certain cult followers. As such, their theories about the Sphinx belong to one of those two parallel avenues of investigation, the one fed by the

The ancient Egyptian elite, from pharaoh down, possessed a sense of responsibility toward the less privileged members of society; the importance of a morally upright life was paramount, as is clear from the ancient Egyptians' funerary beliefs.

Although the original significance of the Great Sphinx remains obscure, it came to be regarded as the guardian of the Giza necropolis.

millennium-old misunderstandings of ancient Egypt. Attempts to date the Sphinx by "scientific" analysis of the stone itself have proved to be quite debatable. The schism between the symbolists' assessment of the Great Sphinx and that of more traditional Egyptologists will continue as long as the general public continues to confuse the symbolists' cultic interpretations of ancient Egypt's culture with rigorously sound, academically proven scientific methods. It is far better to look at the ancient Egyptian records themselves in order to see what the ancient Egyptians had to say about their own civilization. In this discussion of the Old Kingdom, the subjects of medicine, already raised as an issue in connection with Imhotop, and mathematics, which one invariably connects with the Great Pyramids at Giza, demand some comment, inasmuch as popular opinion maintains that the ancient Egyptians were skilled physicians and sophisticated mathematicians. Let us examine each subject in turn.

The ancient Egyptians' understanding of medicine and mathematics was often combined with elements of superstition or religious ritual, owing much to potions and incantations.

It is often maintained that the ancient Egyptians developed a deep understanding of the physiology of the human body as a result of their development of the processes of mummification. In point of fact, nothing could be further from the truth. During the course of mummification, the human brain was regarded as of little consequence and was immediately discarded upon removal from the skull. The male reproductive system was imperfectly understood because the ancient Egyptians linked fluid in the spine with semen. The heart was considered the seat of intelligence rather than the organ which controlled the circulatory system. From these and other examples it becomes clear that ancient Egyptian medicine was not as state-of-the-art as some would have us believe. Many ailments were attributed to the malevolent intervention of evil and these could be removed only by the application of magical potions administered with the proper recitation of appropriate spells.

On the other hand, in certain pragmatic instances, the ancient Egyptians did distinguish themselves as competent physicians (pages 77 and 166-167). The Edwin Smith Surgical Papyrus, now in the collections of the New York Academy of Medicine, deals with wounds to the head and thorax, apparently of types received by soldiers in battle, and is quite sober in its assessment of how to treat each one listed. In some cases, the diagnosis recognizes that the wound is terminal, and the comfort of the patient in his final hours is recommended. The Ebers Papyrus, now in Leipzig, contains very practical information about the treatment of boils and cysts, and other papyri deal in significant ways with gynecological conditions. After an examination of all such papyri to have survived, it may be stated quite frankly that, as time passed, ancient Egyptian medical practices relied increasingly on potions and incantations (page 77).

Just as ancient Egyptian medical papyri have survived, so too have ancient Egyptian mathematical papyri. Of these perhaps none is more famous than the Rhind Mathematical Papyrus, the major portion of which is in London's British Museum, although there are also fragments belonging to this same scroll in The Brooklyn Museum in New York City. Recent investigations suggest that the contents of this document go back to the Pyramid Age of the Old Kingdom. Its title is written in red ink at the beginning of the document and translates as the "correct method of reckoning, for grasping the meaning of things and knowing everything that is, obscurities... and all secrets." Such a title would delight the symbolists, but what follows is sadly disappointing in that regard because the papyrus takes the form of a textbook which states mathematical problems verbally and then suggests how to arrive at the solutions. Three sample problems in this papyrus deal with how to compute the area of a circle. The directions for finding the solution are simply stated and require the mathematician to subtract one ninth of the length from the circle's diameter and square the result. Nowhere is there any indication whatsoever that the ancient Egyptian mathematicians developed the concept of the irrational number π. Nevertheless, their computations were extremely accurate and, when compared with modern calculations to solve the same problem, result in errors of less than 0.6%. Such accuracy was the best ever achieved in the ancient world before the development of Greek mathematics.

With the beginning of Dynasty 5, the society of ancient Egypt was transformed. Pharaoh was somewhat less divine than he had been earlier and was now recognized as the son of Re, the sun god. Pharaoh, who had heretofore required no specially carved spells in his sepulcher to insure him of resurrection in the hereafter, now needed an elaborate series of religious inscriptions, termed the Pyramid Texts, which were inscribed within the burial chambers of some pyramids beginning with the reign of Unas, the last king of Dynasty 5. The building of earlier pyramids appears to have caused the redistribution of the wealth of the land. Pharaoh became less wealthy because of those expenditures; other members of the elite were proportionately enriched. By the end of Dynasty 5 more and more members of the enriched elite, ensconced in various places throughout the land, openly challenged the position of pharaoh. Some kings, such as Titi of Dynasty 6, in order to avert a challenge to their authority, married their daughters to high officials in an effort to maintain the status quo. On other occasions the challenge came from within the harem, as happened when one of the wives of pharaoh Pipi I of Dynasty 6 conspired to assassinate him. The threats apparently continued, so that late in his reign this same pharaoh married in succession two daughters of the official of Abydos, ostensibly to avert another assault on his position.

Throughout this period the members of the elite continued to acquire wealth, often at the expense of pharaoh himself. The political situation at this time has been rightly compared to the situation in the Predynastic Period, when ambitious members of the elite emerged as leaders of local enclaves and gradually extended their power over the territories of their neighbors. The situation apparently reached crisis proportions during the reign of Pipi II of Dynasty 6, who, according to tradition, ruled for over ninety years, although in truth his reign may not have lasted more than thirty three years – still a long time when measured by the standards of the day. He apparently outlived many of his heirs and was unable to curb the power of the local elites, whose wealth, to judge from their tombs, was enormous. Upon his death he was succeeded by a son who ruled for less than a year. He was followed by Queen Nitocris, who ruled Egypt in her own right as a woman and bore the title King of Upper and Lower Egypt. By then, however, the fabric of Egypt had begun to unravel. Soon local dynasts began to compete with one another in their individual attempts to become king of the land. This episode of anarchy is termed the First Intermediate Period, and from its warring factions would emerge the Middle Kingdom.

This bleak picture of the political dissolution and the absolute break down of royal, central authority at the close of the Old Kingdom often overshadows some of the important accomplishments of Dynasties 5 and 6. Foremost among these is an Egyptian presence in lands far removed from the Nile Valley. The kings of these dynasties dispatched military missions to the south into what is now termed Kush, or Nubia, and left inscriptions in the region in which they relate their subjugation of the area. The objective of such campaigns was to control the trade routes by which the riches of Africa might be funnelled into Egypt. These goods included, according to contemporary texts, ebony, panther

In Dynasty 5, pharaoh began to lose his aura of invincibility; members of the elite started to challenge his authority.

skins, and elephant tusks. Pipi II was entertained by the dances of a pygmy who had been brought to Egypt. So apprehensive was he about the well-being of the pygmy that he ordered, according to a preserved inscription, *men to watch over him when he was on board the vessel transporting him to Egypt lest he fall overboard... others to surround his tent at night when he slept during which time they were to check in on him at specific intervals.*

Pharaohs of these dynasties launched campaigns against the Libyans to the west. They also dispatched vessels to distant ports. Some plied the Red Sea to the land of Punt, thought to be located in the territory of the modern nation state of Somalia, in order to obtain the myrrh so necessary for the incense used in religious celebrations; while others sailed to Byblos in The Lebanon in order to obtain cedar, and there in the forests the ancient Egyptians appear to have encountered the bear for the first time. It was during this time as well that the first documented contacts between Egypt and the lands which are part of the modern nation state of Greece were established. A stone vessel inscribed with the name of Weserkaef, the first king of Dynasty 5, was discovered on the Aegean island of Kythera.

The First Intermediate Period signalled the end of the Old Kingdom and its incomparable achievements. Egypt began to break up into warring factions, from which emerged the Middle Kingdom.

Statue of Pharaoh Khaefre, enthroned
(detail, left) **Old Kingdom, Dynasty 4**
Alabaster; 31 1/2" in height
Findspot disputed, either Memphis
or Sakkara; CG 41

Khaefre, the pharaoh who ordered the
construction of both the second
pyramid on the Giza Plateau as well as
the Great Sphinx, is here represented
dressed in a kilt and nemes headdress.
His attributes include a false beard,
which symbolically imbues him with
strength and virility, and a folded bolt
of cloth which he holds like a
handkerchief in his balled right fist. In
keeping with ancient Egyptian design
tenets, the symmetry of the statue is
varied ever so slightly by the position
of that hand.

One of the more striking observations
about the representations of ancient
Egyptian pharaohs is their noticeable
avoidance of elaborate trappings of
office. When one compares this image
of Khaefre, for example, with that of
a near contemporary, Nefer (page
51), one realizes that the only major
differences between the appearance of
pharaoh and a member of the elite are
the false beard and headdress, and the
appearance of the uraeus, or cobra, on
the brow of the representation of the
pharaoh. Both wear a kilt, the styles
of which are of course different, and
both are bare-chested. This similarity
artistically links pharaoh to the elite,
of which he is a part, and is in stark

contrast to the depiction of monarchs
in other civilizations, both ancient
and modern, who are prone to be
represented heavily dressed in the
costume, accessories, and decorations
of kingship.

Those who claim that the Great
Sphinx at Giza cannot be a depiction
of Khaefre because the face of that
beast, despite its damaged state, does
not resemble known statues of
Khaefre, such as this, are
inappropriately applying axioms
of Western art history to the study
of ancient Egyptian art. Images
in ancient Egypt are expressions of
ideology, not portraits in the Western
sense. As a result, one would expect
differences in the depictions of any
given pharaoh.

This statue is also of interest to
scholars, because the circumstances

of its discovery are a matter of
controversy. According to the sources
cited at the time of its acquisition
by the Egyptian Museum, the statue
is said to have been discovered at
Memphis, Sakkara, or Giza. This
confusion has led some scholars to
suggest, at least informally, that the
statue may be a forgery, created in the
1880s, when it first appeared. Other
scholars maintain that the statue may
have been created at a later time
during the Old Kingdom in memory
of Khaefre. These suggestions are
presented here to alert the visitor
to the fact that scholars often differ
markedly in their assessments of
ancient Egyptian works of art.

Striding statue of Nefer,
Director of Brewers
Old Kingdom, Dynasty 5
Painted limestone; 13 3/4" in height
From Sakkara; CG 145

This statuette is instructive from several points of view. Nefer is represented in a striding pose, with his left leg advanced. Despite what local guides may tell tourists, the reason the left leg is advanced in ancient Egyptian art has nothing to do with the observation that modern armies traditionally step off with their left feet or with the suggestion that the left foot is anatomically closer to the heart. This particular attitude in sculpture in the round is explained by the fact that ancient Egyptian art is rooted in the hieroglyphs, as a comparison with the two-dimensional painted relief of Hekaib (detail, left), although dated to a later period, reveals. In such representations, primacy of place is reserved for that part of the relief which is to the spectator's left. Consequently, the left-hand image of Hekaib depicts him holding the baton of office which passes in front of his kilt. Compare this detail to the entire relief (pages 84-85) and one will immediately see that the right-hand image of Hekaib represents him holding that same baton which there passes behind him. When the ancient Egyptian craftsmen began to craft statues they realized that the most important pose in a two-dimensional scene was the left-most pose.

There, as the previous discussion has just shown, the figure is represented with the left leg advanced. That pose and that forward leg were then retained for sculpture, which can profitably be regarded as a translation into three dimensions of a two-dimensional image.

Secondly, the torso of Nefer is rendered in what art historians term bipartition, that is, his torso is depicted as two, symmetrically vertical components. In reality, however, the male torso is anatomically characterized by tripartition; its component elements are the lower abdomen, the rib cage, and the region of the pectoral muscles. The fact that ancient Egyptian craftsmen habitually failed to render the nude male torso in accordance with its anatomically correct components should caution one against interpreting such art literally.

Finally, the ancient Egyptian craftsmen wanted their audience to understand that the negative stone, that is the stone which was part of the original block from which the statue was made, was not part of the subject depicted. Consequently, that stone is painted black.

**Statue of Sekedkau,
Inspector of the Scribes of the
Sealed Documents, together with
his wife and son, enthroned
Old Kingdom, Dynasty 5
Painted limestone; 20 1/2" in height
From Sakkara; CG 101**

The first thing one notices in this statue is the remarkable state of the paint's preservation, which is almost as fresh today as it was nearly four thousand years ago when it was originally applied. Sekedkau, to the right, and his wife, in the center, sit upon a highbacked chair, which differs from the thrones of Khaefre (page 49) and Iris (pages 56-57). In keeping with ancient Egyptian artistic conventions, the symmetry of their bodies is broken by the subtly different attitudes of their arms. Their feet are shown parallel to one another, because they are depicted as seated. On the other hand, the left leg of their son, to the left, is advanced in keeping with the time-honored convention for the depiction of the striding male figure (pages 50-51). The garments worn by the members of this family are painted white, as a convention indicating the linen from which they were woven. Linen, unlike wool, has no natural mordants by which dyes might remain color-fast in the fabric. The white kilts of the father and son represent that linen in its undyed state. The dress of the wife and mother is, by way of contrast, heavily painted in the area of the bodice. Whether this paint is intended to represent a pattern dyed into the fabric is questionable, because of the nature of linen. It is far more likely, as recent studies of ancient Egyptian textiles suggest, that the patterns on that bodice were actually hand-painted on to the dress. Accordingly, the dress had to be repainted after each laundering.

There is, however, some debate about whether such tightly fitting sheaths as that worn by Sekedkau's wife were actually worn in life. The debate is not academic since actual examples of such dresses have been found by archaeologists. Because these garments are not made of stretchable material, such as a modern spandex, and are not provided with fasteners, modern fashion models, when called in to assist Egyptologists, have been unable to get into these dresses; they were unable to get the garment over their arms and shoulders. For this reason, such sheaths are perhaps better regarded as dresses reserved for death, rather than as the staple of the well-dressed Egyptian woman's wardrobe. All members of this family are shown wearing similar accessories, the most prominent element of which is the broad collar. Unisex jewelry, therefore, is not a phenomenon restricted to the 1990s.

**Statue of Iris, Greatest of the Ten
of Upper Egypt and Prophet of Maat,
Goddess of Truth, enthroned**
(pages 56-57)
**Old Kingdom, Dynasty 5
Silicified sandstone (?)
15 3/4" in height
From Sakkara; CG 131**

Since ancient Egyptian art is the visual
expression of certain societal values,
the attitudes in which rulers and
members of the elite are depicted
were consciously selected for their
symbolic value. Iris is depicted
enthroned, a statue type which was
originally reserved during the Archaic
Period exclusively for pharaohs.
As the position of king diminished
during the course of the Old
Kingdom, more and more officials
elected to be represented in such an
enthroned attitude, which proclaimed
that the gap separating them from
pharaoh had closed. The elevated
status which such enthroned statues
imparted was maintained throughout
the course of Egyptian history. As
a result, some of the very last statues
ever created in ancient Egypt during
the first century A.D. habitually
depict members of the elite in similar
enthroned poses (page 213).

**Statue of Nymaatsed, Priest of the
God Amun and of Goddess Hathor,
as well as Prophet of the Pyramids
of the Pharaohs of Dynasty 5
Old Kingdom, Dynasty 5
Painted granite; 17" in height
From Sakkara; CG 58**

The tomb of Nymaatsed, located
to the east of the Step Pyramid
of pharaoh Djoser at Sakkara, was
discovered late in the last century by
Auguste Mariette, whose own tomb
lies against the western wall of the
garden of the Egyptian Museum
in Cairo. Mariette was a responsible
Egyptologist whose guiding principles
laid the foundation not only for the
future Egyptian Museum but for the
archaeological service as well. He
was also the individual who provided
the story line for Verdi's *Aïda*,
based on his translation of ancient
texts recounting the exploits of the
pharaohs of Dynasty 26 against
the Kushites.

The granite statue of Nymaatsed
depicts him seated on the ground,
cross-legged in an attitude generally
reserved for scribes. Such a position
naturally stretches the fabric of the
kilt taut so that it forms a convenient
table-top on which to unroll a
papyrus. Such a papyrus, indicated

in paint, is in fact represented lying
on top of his stretched kilt.
Nymaatsed's head is slightly raised
and his eyes are intensely focused,
as if he is carefully listening to
the instructions he is receiving from
a superior.

The state of the paint's preservation
is remarkable. Paint has been used
to indicate not only the papyrus
on his lap, but also his broad collar,
and facial features which include the
presence of a neatly trimmed
moustache. The tuck of fabric to the
left of the navel is a subtle way in
which the craftsmen responsible for
this statue varied the strict symmetry
of the sculpture.

**False Door of Seankhenptah,
Director of Metal-Workers
Old Kingdom, Dynasty 6
Limestone; 41" in height
From Sakkara; CG 1445**

The original function of this false
door, within a tomb at Sakkara, was
to enable the deceased magically to
move to and fro from the tomb to the
offerings in order that his *ka,* or spirit,
might be adequately provisioned.
In order to reinforce the function to
which this architectural element was
put, the craftsmen customarily
included a rectangular tablet above
the central recess, which symbolically
represented the door itself, on which
the deceased was often shown
seated before a well-supplied
offering table. The inscriptions
there, as well as in vertical columns
elsewhere on the false door,
contain the names and titles of the
deceased in addition to a version
of the offering formula itself. The
tablet and inscriptions symbolically
assured the deceased's *ka* of the
necessary provisions in the
hereafter, regardless of whether
the living performed the necessary
rituals on his behalf and brought
along the required items.
Several mirror images of the
deceased are often included on the
jambs of the false door, and these
sometimes represent him at two
different ages in life. One image
is more youthful and vigorous,
whereas the second is older and
portly. The intention of such
juxtapositions is to provide visual
documentation of the deceased's
progress up the bureaucratic
ladder, a process of change which
was thought to continue even after
death, as the deceased made his
way into the hereafter only to be
resurrected as a child.

**Statue of Moses
and his wife, Semerka
Old Kingdom, Dynasty 5
Painted limestone; 29" in height
From Giza; JE 38670**

Moses, a fairly common proper name
throughout the history of ancient
Egypt, is depicted with all of the
ancient Egyptian conventions for the
striding male figure. His balled fists
each hold an object, which has been
convincingly described as a folded
bolt of cloth, not unlike that held as
a handkerchief by Khaefre (page 49).
The bilateral symmetry of his pose is
broken, as expected, only by the tuck
of his kilt which appears to the left of
his navel. His broad collar resembles
that worn by his wife, whose tightly
fitting sheath is better regarded as the
dress of death. In addition, she wears
an elaborate wig.
In keeping with certain artistic
conventions, the skin tones of Moses
are a brownish-red, indicative, it has
been argued, of his activities which
were conducted out-of-doors. His
wife's are yellow, indicative of her ideal
seclusion within their home. To argue,
therefore, as some have done about
the ethnicity of the ancient Egyptians
relying solely on the appearance
of such skin colors is bound to have
disastrous results. Few would, for
example, argue that Semerka was an
oriental on the basis of her skin color.
Polychromy in ancient Egyptian art
is symbolic, not representational.
In addition, one notes the use of black
paint, a convention in the Old
Kingdom intended to mask the
negative stone and separate it from the
principal images.
This pair statue exhibits a very
interesting feature which may be taken
as representative of ancient Egyptian
culture as a whole. The wife, and not
the husband, is the supporting figure.
Her left arm reaches around his torso
in an embrace as she steadies herself
by placing her right hand on his
forearm. The pose appears to be
indebted to that first developed for
statues of pharaoh Menkaure of
Dynasty 4, in which he is habitually
shown in just such a protective
embrace of a goddess.

THE MIDDLE KINGDOM

Previous page
The Pyramid of Pharaoh
Amunemhat III at Hawara
Middle Kingdom, Dynasty 12
The reign of Amunemhat III marks the return of the status quo to ancient Egyptian history because the members of the elite, after an interval of rivalry, came to recognize the supremacy of pharaoh in Egyptian society. Doubtless because both he and his predecessors had embarked on extensive land reclamation projects in the Faiyum, Amunemhat III chose this garden-like setting as the location of his pyramid and final resting place. The pyramid, constructed of a mudbrick core, was originally faced with stone which was removed over the ages by the hand of man; it rose to a height of just under 200 feet, and was anciently called "Amunemhat lives." The pyramid was erected alongside the Bahr Yousef, clearly visible in this view, which brought water from the Nile River into the Faiyum. Tradition maintains that this irrigation canal was constructed under the direction of the Hebrew patriarch Joseph during his sojourn in Egypt as pharaoh's chief administrator; hence the Arabic form of its name. In point of fact scholars are uncertain about when this particular channel was actually dug.

The mortuary temple which served the needs of the cult of the deceased Amunemhat III lies immediately to the south of the pyramid. It was so large that the ancient Greeks, comparing it to the legendary maze erected on Crete by their King Minos, called it the Labyrinth. It was skillfully constructed of granite so finely joined together that the joins between the courses seemed to disappear. As a result, some Greeks were led to the mistaken conclusion that the entire complex had been carved out of the rock of a single small mountain. Little remains of this vast complex, which is said to have consisted of some 3,000 individual rooms, save for granite fragments which still protrude here and there from the field on which this enormous edifice once stood.

The collapse of the Old Kingdom was followed by the First Intermediate Period, lasting approximately a century and a half, during which time Egypt's society was characterized by anarchy and chaos. Certain members of the elite, whose families had profited during the course of Dynasties 5 and 6, now gained the ascendancy, whereas others, having lost their advantaged stations in life, plunged into obscurity. The social deck of Egypt had in a real sense been shuffled and dealt anew. And whilst that reshuffling did seriously affect the lives of almost every individual at each level of society, it did not alter the fundamental principle upon which ancient Egyptian civilization rested. Namely, the institutions which gave the elite their advantaged positions in society remained in place; the only change was to the composition of that elite.

Several literary texts have survived from those tumultuous times which clearly indicate the topsy-turvy nature of ancient Egyptian society during the First Intermediate Period. These texts, which seem to have been written from the perspective of those whose fortunes had soured, relate with contempt how the mighty had fallen and the lowly risen. The Lamentations of Iperwer typically express these sentiments: *Behold, those who were once the owners of fine robes now go about in rags whereas others who never possessed a shirt now sport about in the finest linen garments...* In dealing with this period, many historians seem to concentrate on the negative aspects of Egyptian society and fail to realize that through it all a marked social conscience habitually punctuates the literature of the period. It is as if the ancient Egyptians did realize that something was terribly wrong with their lives. They understood the meaning of social injustice.

One turns again to the Lamentations of Iperwer and to a treatise called the Prophecy of Neferti in order to find such sentiments eloquently expressed: *Children, which many parents long to have, are now randomly abandoned on the high ground... If three men set out on a thoroughfare together, only two arrive at the final destination. The greater number kills the lesser... What a pyramid once hid has now become empty... Men rob stones from the tombs of those of bygone ages in order to reuse that material for their own tombs...*

Reprehensible activities such as child abuse, aggravated assault, murder, robbery, the looting of tombs, both royal and private, and the like appear to have been routine occurrences during the First Intermediate Period. But the fact that some Egyptians witnessed such socially unacceptable behavior and wrote about it in these terms forcefully demonstrates to those of us living in this century that the ancient Egyptians did know the difference between right and wrong. The inherent difficulty, however, was how to bring an end to such abuses, as made abundantly clear in the Dispute over Suicide, in which the anonymous hero, talking to his conscience, contemplates taking his own life because he senses the futility of trying to reform the wicked society in which he is living: *To whom can I speak today [about these abuses]? I am despondent because I have no like-minded friend. Really, to whom can I speak today? The sin which permeates society today has no end!* The Dispute, however, ends on an optimistic note because the hero becomes convinced that fighting against injustice is far better than just giving up.

Toward the end of the First Intermediate Period some semblance of law and order, at least on a local level, was restored when the elite in several different cities consolidated their respective positions by relying on the military forces they had been developing. The long and protracted struggles between these competing local elites, often in the form of bloody military contests, would eventually result in the reunification of Egypt. One of the competing elite groups during this time was centered in the city of Herakleopolis, and its ruler,

Merekare, aware of the disjunctions in society, formulated a series of maxims by which his rule was governed. He passed this advice, which acknowledges the importance of members of the elite, on to his son in a treatise known as the Instructions of Pharaoh Merekare: *Promote the great men (i.e. those now part of the elite) in your realm so that they may carry out your laws... Great is a great man when his men are great... Valiant is the king possessed of courtiers; august is the monarch who is rich in his nobles.*

The social deck had indeed been reshuffled. A newly constituted elite had emerged, and its members were now being pressed into service as co-opted members loyally serving their local monarch in the hope that he might some day become pharaoh of all of Egypt, and that they might then share in the benefits of that outcome. One such official, Ankhtifi by name, was nomarch, or provincial governor, of the city of Hierakonpolis. He was a loyal supporter of the ruler of Herakleopolis, who is suggested to have been Neferkare VII. Among the inscriptions in his tomb at Moalla in Upper Egypt, Ankhtifi records his role in the military conflict between his sovereign and the forces of the opposition elite which were centered in the city of Thebes: *I went downstream... and found that all of the rival forces of Thebes... had attacked the town of Armant. Then I reached the west bank of the Theban province... my courageous crack troops ventured to the west and east of this Theban province, looking for an open battle. But no one dared to come out from Thebes because they were afraid of my troops...*

In addition to being a military leader, Ankhtifi prides himself on exhibiting outstanding social qualities. He unabashedly states: *The whole of Upper Egypt died of hunger and each individual had reached such a state of hunger that he ate his own children. But I refused to see anyone die of hunger in this province. I arranged for grain to be loaned to Upper Egypt and gave to the north the grain of Upper Egypt... I brought life to the provinces... I was the man who found the solution when it was lacking in the country...*

The competing local elites, while engaged in bloody armed conflicts with their neighbors, had nevertheless managed to restore some semblance of equilibrium to the territories under their control. The local dynasts and members of their newly formed elite, as this extract suggests, did succeed in restoring to their domains that characteristically ancient Egyptian ethos which mandated the well-being of the less fortunate. After a series of perennial military struggles, the elites of the cities of Herakleopolis and of Thebes emerged victorious, and they now warred with one another in an attempt to unify the two lands and proclaim one of their members pharaoh of all of Egypt. A winner finally emerged in the person of Montuhotep Nebhepetere (pages 70-71) who finally succeeded in unifying the two lands for the first time since the collapse of the Old Kingdom.

An intimate glimpse into the very human lives of the ancient Egyptians during Dynasty 11 is provided by a series of personal letters, written on papyrus, and now in the collections of The Metropolitan Museum of Art in New York City, which are known as the Hekanakht Archive, after the name of the head of the family who penned them. Hekanakht had five sons. He kept the eldest on a short leash and held him responsible for everything that went wrong with the family's enterprises: *As to the flooding that is occurring on our land, you are the one who is cultivating it... I shall hold you personally responsible for any damages!* He was apparently overly indulgent toward his youngest son who could do no wrong in his father's eyes and often behaved irresponsibly: *If he has no allowance, do not fail to write to me about it. I have been told that he is very unhappy.*

Hekanakht also had a concubine on whom he doted endlessly. When a third son and a household maid attempted to paint this concubine in a very bad light,

The confusion and disorder in Egyptian society which accompanied the First Intermediate Period, preceding the Middle Kingdom, is revealed in literary texts of the time: "One man takes the property of another and gives it to a total stranger."

Hekanakht demanded that: *...the household maid be turned out of my house immediately. If she spends a single day in that house when my concubine visits it, you will bear the full brunt of the consequences! You'd better listen to my warning, so that no harm comes to my concubine, do you understand?*

Because this archive only contains those letters which have survived, one cannot determine how this family feud was eventually resolved. But the mystery writer Agatha Christie had a few ideas of her own on this matter, and presented them in her novel, Death Comes as the End, which is based on the Hekanakht Archive.

Whereas the military conquest of the Theban kings did restore the central authority of Egypt after the turbulent First Intermediate Period, it was not able to curb the ambitions of the elite, whose members repeatedly attempted to assert themselves at the expense of pharaoh. This often resulted in assassination plots against the pharaoh himself. Amunemhat I, the founder of Dynasty 12, was the victim of just such a plot. He had risen to the rank of pharaoh after having served as vizier, one of the highest officials of the land, under the last pharaohs of Dynasty 11. Although the identify of the assassins has not been preserved, their immediate goals do not seem to have been achieved, because Amunemhat I was succeeded by his son, Senuseret I, whom historians do not seem to implicate in the conspiracy.

The pharaohs of Dynasty 12 were confronted, therefore, with a very peculiar problem. They were dependent on the cooperation of the members of the elite for the smooth operation of their government, but they realized full well that those same individuals were their rivals, often resorting to murder. The Instructions of Amunemhat I, purportedly written before his assassination, but more probably composed shortly after his death by those sympathetic with the plight of pharaoh, clearly articulates the dilemma confronting the kings of Dynasty 12: *Keep yourself aloof from those subordinate to you... do not approach them in your loneliness... whenever you sleep, you yourself must be your own best bodyguard...* And yet the pharaoh, in this same treatise, is aware of his social responsibilities: *I did give to the destitute and raised the orphan... I enabled the one who had nothing to become someone...*

As a result of such an endemic dilemma, some art historians have looked at the faces of the pharaohs of Dynasty 12 and recognized in them certain features, termed signs of age, which imbue those faces with what is easily interpreted as careworn, worried expressions (pages 68-69 and 75). As a result, some have applied Shakespeare's line, "heavy is the heart that wears the crown," to these images.

Such interpretations, persuasive as they may appear at first glance, are in fact based on an imperfect understanding of the role of the elite vis-à-vis pharaoh during Dynasty 12. Recent art historical study has demonstrated that such haggard faces appear earlier on statues of officials, that is on the faces of the members of the elite, than on the faces of pharaohs of the Middle Kingdom (page 82). The choice of a different "look" was intentional and was meant to demonstrate that the members of the elite were artistically distancing themselves from their monarchs, just as in life they were competing with the monarchs for power. In an effort to diminish this artistic difference between pharaoh and the members of the elite, the kings of Dynasty 12 decided to follow that lead and were subsequently represented with the same signs of age on the faces of their images. Such images are, therefore, to be interpreted as artistic manifestations of a political ideology and are never to be termed portraits.

The Theban kings restored a semblance of order during the Middle Kingdom, but ambitious members of the elite continued to challenge pharaoh. The careworn images of the pharaohs of Dynasty 12 are less a reflection of these turbulent times, more the manifestations of political ideology.

By the time of pharaoh Amunemhat III (pages 68-69 and 75) the members of the elite appear to have accepted the reality of pharaoh's preeminent position in society, as is evident from the Instructions written by one of his treasury officials to his own children: *I am revealing to you something important. Listen! Worship pharaoh... within your bodies and associate with his majesty in your hearts... He gives food to those who are in his service, and provisions those who tread his path... be scrupulous in your oaths to him that you may be free from the taint of disloyalty...*

Despite the competition early in the dynasty between the king and members of the elite, the pharaohs of the Middle Kingdom may be judged to have been effective rulers of Egypt, particularly in agricultural matters. They realized that the height of the annual flood of the Nile affected the yield of the farmers' crops. A Nile which was too high was just as damaging as one which was too low. As a result, these pharaohs dispatched surveyors deep into the reaches of the Nile to the south of Aswan where they could monitor the size of the on-coming flood in order to prepare the administrators of the land for any eventuality.

These same pharaohs fostered huge land reclamation projects, particularly in the Faiyum, a great geological depression southwest of modern Cairo (pages 60-61). By one estimate, the agricultural activities of these pharaohs in this region placed an additional 27,000 acres of arable land under cultivation each year.

Preoccupied with trade and with securing the frontiers of Egypt, these pharaohs erected enormous forts along the Nile to the south of Aswan. The forts not only kept the local populations in check, they also enabled the Egyptians to control the luxury goods passing from the more southerly reaches of Africa into Egypt.

No discussion of the Middle Kingdom can be complete without saying a few words about the language and the literature of the period. For many scholars, the hieroglyphs of the Middle Kingdom represent the high-water mark of the ancient Egyptian scribe's craft (pages 80-81 and 84-85). Each sign is generally well carved and very neatly situated within the space allocated to it. As a result, students today in Egyptology graduate programs worldwide are trained in drawing hieroglyphs by copying these signs from the Middle Kingdom.

But the scribes of the Middle Kingdom were not simply consummate draughtsmen. They were wonderful authors whose works were so admired by later generations of ancient Egyptians that they became classics, repeatedly copied as school exercises by an endless succession of ancient Egyptian students. That tradition continues to this day because advanced graduate students in Egyptology are first introduced to the intricacies of ancient Egyptian grammar, syntax, and vocabulary by translating into English, or another modern language, many of these same texts. The literature of the Middle Kingdom serves, therefore, as a model of the ancient Egyptian language, just as Julius Caesar's Gallic War is an appropriate model for the study of Latin. The following are synopses of three classic examples of Middle Kingdom literature.

The Tale of the Eloquent Peasant is an interesting account of ancient Egyptian justice. It begins with a fieldhand who is about to bid his wife and children goodbye as he loads his donkey with the produce of his farm. The description of the quantities and variety of that produce laden on the poor beast is intended to evoke laughter, but anyone traveling in the Middle East today will soon realize that donkeys are in fact still loaded to overflowing in much this same manner.

Soon the fieldhand is on his way and is seen by a jealous official who covets the fieldhand's belongings. He muses, "would that I had an efficacious idol with which to gain possession of that fieldhand's chattel." In an attempt to gain his wish, the official purposefully obstructs the path on which the donkey must travel. In order to avoid the obstacle, the donkey deviates from the path and enters a corner of the official's wheat field. Thereupon a stalk of wheat brushes up against the donkey's mouth. He eats it. The official then claims that the fieldhand turned his donkey loose into his fields to graze. He demands compensation. The fieldhand attempts to explain what actually happened, but his explanation is of no avail.

Undaunted, the fieldhand begins to plead his case, traveling from one jurisdiction to another in the hope of obtaining justice. His persistence eventually enables him to plead his case before pharaoh himself. He argues his case so eloquently that pharaoh is moved, and justice is served. The charges are dropped.

The moral of this tale is that any ancient Egyptian, regardless of his station in life, could theoretically seek redress of a grievance from pharaoh himself. Pharaoh was the law. It is for that reason, perhaps, that the ancient Egyptians did not develop written law codes, such as those found in Mesopotamia, of which that of Hammurabi, king of Babylon about 1750 B.C., is perhaps the best known. More importantly, however, it demonstrates once again that the masses were well-served by the system established by the elite at the dawn of ancient Egypt's history.

Of all of the classics of ancient Egyptian literature perhaps none was more popular than the Tale of Sinuhe, which is set during the beginning of Dynasty 12 and opens with the assassination of Amunemhat I, the reporting of which is overheard by Sinuhe, the hero. Fearing that he will be implicated in the plot, although he is innocent, Sinuhe opts to flee Egypt as an exile. His journeys bring him to the Syria-Palestine region where he is befriended by an Asiatic sheikh. The term "Asiatic" is traditionally employed in Egyptological literature to designate an inhabitant of the area generally known today as the Middle East. Sinuhe's encounter with these Asiatics is very informative, because one reads for the very first time in Egyptian sources themes which are parallel to narratives in the Old Testament. So, for example, Sinuhe, champions his adopted tribe against a rival, but does so in an interesting manner. In order to avoid an armed confrontation among all the male members of both tribes, a decision is reached whereby each tribe will be represented by one warrior. These two will then do battle in a duel. The ensuing contest has all of the hallmarks of the famous encounter between David and Goliath, so much so that in the end Sinuhe, although he did not use a sling, nevertheless beheads his adversary, who, like Goliath, is described as being of gigantic size.

Sinuhe wins the hand of the sheikh's daughter in marriage and prospers, growing old in his adopted homeland. He yearns to return to Egypt, but fears that he is still a wanted man. In the end, Sinuhe is invited to return, and all is forgiven. Like Odysseus at the end of his travels, Sinuhe is now returned to his beloved Egypt. There he is eventually buried in what is described as an opulent tomb, lavishly equipped with funerary furnishings and complete with a garden. This story has staying power for the West because it was adapted during the course of World War II into an historical novel, The Egyptian, by Mika Waltari. That novel served in turn as the basis for the 1954 Hollywood movie of the same name, which starred Jean Simmons and Victor Mature and featured Edmund Purdom in the lead role.

The Story of the Shipwrecked Sailor is perhaps the most fanciful of the classics of the Middle Kingdom. In keeping with the ancient Egyptian love of anonymity, the hero of the tale, a brave sea captain, gathers a crew of hearty sailors in preparation for his forthcoming voyage. As he boards his vessel, the narrative boasts

The hieroglyphs of the Middle Kingdom attained new heights of draftsmanship; the literature of the period is studied even today.

**Statue of Pharaoh Amunemhat III
as a Sphinx** (pages 68-69)
**Middle Kingdom, Dynasty 12
Gray granite; 35 1/2" in length
From Tell Basta (Bubastis); JE 87082**

The realistic looking features on
the face of this king have traditionally
been interpreted as external signs of
introspection and heaviness of heart
associated with the burdens of the
monarchy. It is now recognized that
such signs of age are visual
manifestations of ideology, and that
members of the elite were the first
to cast their facial features in such an
idiom (page 75). They did so in
order to distance themselves from the
pharaohs with whom they were
competing for power.

The ancient Greek word, sphinx,
is used to describe a composite beast,
which the ancient Egyptians often
termed a "living image," because
it embodied the strength and power
of a lion, the qualities of which were
then symbolically transferred to the
pharaoh whose head it bore. In the
case of this particular representation,
the significance of the lion may be
extended to include characteristics of
the goddess Bastet, because the statue
was discovered in 1943 at Bubastis
in the vicinity of her temple there.
Whereas the animal traditionally
associated with Bastet is indeed a cat,
her nature was often conflated with
that of Sekhmet (pages 96-97).
In certain instances, therefore, both
Bastet and Sekhmet, as lionesses, were
possessed of savage powers capable
of destruction.

This sphinx was once part of a dyad,
or pair statue, consisting of two
figures, the second originally
appearing on the spectator's left-hand
side, as the break indicates. One
might, therefore, tentatively suggest
a restoration of the goddess Bastet in
that position, indicating that the king,
by virtue of placating the redoubtable
goddess, has gained both her
protection and might.

In contrast to composite beasts in
Western cultures, such as Halloween
monsters, which are meant to frighten
us through the ungainly ways in which
their disparate body parts are joined,
Egyptian composite beasts appear
rather unthreatening to Western
sensibilities. That perceived effect may
be ascribed to the fundamental design
principles governing the hieroglyphs,
which themselves admit of composite
signs. As expected, the zone of
transition between the human head
of the pharaoh and the animal body
of the lion has been neatly masked
by the mane, the tufts of which frame
the face as if they were a kind
of broad collar (pages 176-177).

that this captain is so sea-savvy that he can foretell a storm before it arrives. The Egyptian word for foretell contains the hieroglyph for a giraffe, which, apparently, can see things before others less tall can. Almost as soon as this statement is made, a storm does in fact blow up and the ship is sunk. The entire crew is lost at sea save for the captain who manages to grab hold of some flotsam which carries him to the shores of a remote, mysterious island. The skipper is amazed to find that the island is a kind of paradise, abounding with fruits and vegetables, fish and fowl, all of which adequately satisfy his hunger.

In the midst of this idyllic splendor he hears a roar louder than any thunder clap ever heard by the ears of man. The ground begins to shake. The source of this commotion is a behemoth-like serpent which makes a beeline for the captain, now prostrate on the earth begging for mercy.

The snake gently picks the captain up in his mouth, the way a cat carries a kitten, and returns to his pit. Depositing him gently on the ground, the snake inquires about how the captain got to his island in the first place. The captain recounts in repetitive detail the events described earlier in the narrative. The serpent is moved by the tragedy and becomes compassionate because he, too, like the skipper, endured a tragedy in his life, which he then recounts in detail.

Bonded by virtue of their respective tragedies, the skipper is emboldened to buy his way off the island by offering all of the goods of Egypt to the serpent in exchange for a way to get back home. The serpent laughs at the offer: "Have you no eyes? Look around you. Whatever could you possibly have in Egypt that I do not already have here on this island?"

The ever gracious serpent does, however, continue and prophesies that on an appointed day a vessel from Egypt will arrive. As predicted, the ship arrives and the captain loads it to the gunnels with all the products of this strange, exotic island, and, bidding the serpent a fond farewell, boards the vessel which heads for the open sea.

In keeping with the best of Hollywood's B-movies, the island then sinks beneath the surface of the waters, never to be seen again. When the skipper finally reaches Egypt, he is granted an audience with pharaoh in which he recounts his adventure. The monarch appears to be unimpressed with the tale, and in fact dismisses it as a mere figment of the captain's imagination.

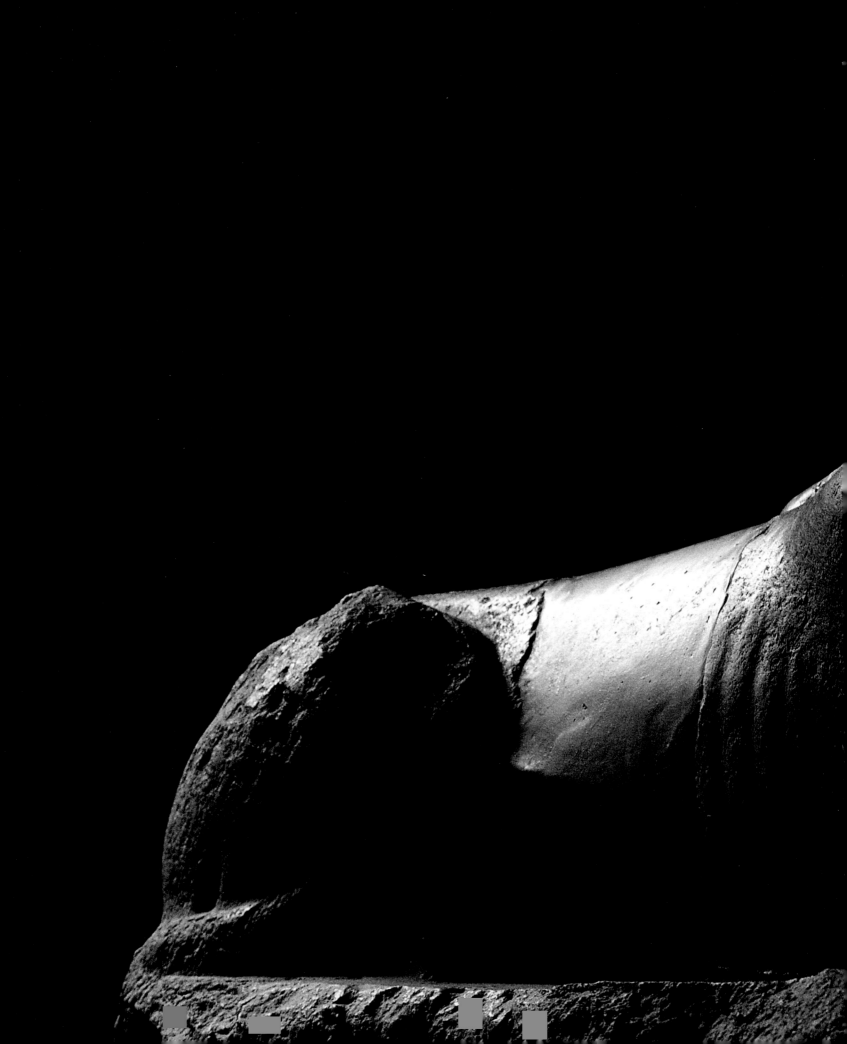

Funerary stela of the scribe, Dedusobek, and his daughter, Renisenebkhonsu
Middle Kingdom, Dynasty 12
Painted limestone; 11" in height
From Abydos; CG 20596

The funerary nature of this stela, or inscribed stone slab, is clearly indicated by its findspot, the northern cemetery at Abydos, as well as by its decoration and accompanying inscriptions. These are painted in blue, a color charged with rejuvenation overtones appropriate for a funerary context, in which the deceased aspires to rebirth in the hereafter. The lunette depicts a Candidae, often identified as a jackal, who is called "the Lord of Abydos, the one who opens the paths [for the deceased to travel upon]." The two principal lines of hieroglyphs contain an abbreviated version of the offering prayer and read: *A boon which the king offers to the god Osiris, foremost of the Westerners, and to the god Ptahsokar so that they may give the sweet breath [of life] to the ka, or spirit, of Dedusobek, the scribe...*
Ancient Egyptian etiquette demanded

that only kings could be granted the breath of life by the gods. As a result, that phrase is disguised in the inscription because the word for "breath" is replaced by a ship's sail, the pronunciation of which punned with that for "breath." The word "life" was understood, and consequently not written. This concealed message is furthered by the accompanying image of Dedusobek who dandles his daughter, Renisenebkhonsu, on his lap. One may tentatively suggest that the familial devotion inherent in such intimate scenes between parents and their children became the precedent upon which similar scenes in the Amarna Period were ultimately based (pages 104-106). Here, Renisenebkhonsu holds a flower to her nose. The flower, like the ship's sail, puns with the phrase for the "breath of life," so that the daughter mimics the role of goddesses who would normally present the king, substituted in this case by her father, with the breath of life. Such veiled references are typical of the art of ancient Egypt, and reveal the elite's

love of puns by which they could circumvent established conventions and appropriate for themselves images and motifs reserved for pharaoh in such subtle ways that their appropriation would not smack of lèse-majesté.
Renisenebkhonsu's youth is emphasized by her hairstyle which has been arranged into a side lock of youth (pages 78-79 and 127), but she wears a dress that both other children and adult women of the period also wear. Her pet dog appears by the chair in which her father sits. The inscriptions mention at least two of her brothers and a sister by name, although they are not shown, and the smaller female figure to the right may be a depiction of her mother, Ankhser.

Relief of Pharaoh Montuhotep Nebhepetere smiting the foe
Middle Kingdom, Dynasty 11
Limestone; 20 1/2" in width
From Gebelein; 1/11/17/10

The period of anarchy and chaos which ushered in the collapse of the Old Kingdom was followed by a protracted period of civil war, during which time members of local elite groups fought with one another for supremacy. In time, the Theban elite, led by Montuhotep Nebhepetere, emerged victorious, and from that victory the Middle Kingdom was born.

At the site of Gebelein in Middle Egypt, Montuhotep Nebhepetere commanded his craftsmen to commemorate his victories over the elite of the north in a series of reliefs, of which this is representative.
The king, wearing the White Crown, emblematic of Upper Egypt, is shown about to smite the foe with his mace. This smiting vignette belongs to a long tradition, at the head of which stands the recto of the Narmer Palette in the Cairo Museum. There, too, the king, wearing the White Crown emblematic of Upper Egypt, is portrayed about to brain the enemy. The constant replication of that one scene throughout the history of ancient Egyptian art is a clear indication that the elite had formulated a single motif, that of pharaoh single-handedly smiting the foe, which so succinctly encompassed pharaoh's role as the annihilator of the forces of chaos, both worldly and mythological, that it was immediately recognized as such without any need for accompanying explicatory texts.
Equally significant is the ancient Egyptian concept of action, as depicted in such scenes. These actions are always representations of potential consequences. The king is always about to smite the foe. He is never shown actually braining the enemy, nor is he shown immediately afterwards, with his weapon dripping with the foe's spent blood. This interest in potential extends to almost every other theme depicted in ancient Egyptian art, and is the most important reason for arguing against the existence of continuous narratives in that art.

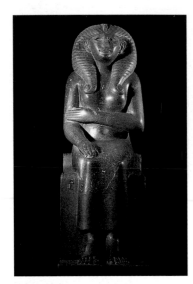

Statue of Queen Neferet, enthroned
Middle Kingdom, Dynasty 12
Gray granite; 65" in height
From Tanis; CG 381

This image of the wife of pharaoh Senuseret II may profitably be regarded as a monumental version of the miniature statuette (page 74), for it exhibits some of the same features. Both women wear a similar sheath, the bodice of which is characterized by the trapezoidal pattern formed by its straps, and both wear the wig associated with the goddess Hathor, with the curls resting on the breasts. There is very little difference, therefore, between the images of queens and those made for non-royal female members of the elite, just as there were only imperceptible differences to a modern's eye between images of pharaoh and his male courtiers (pages 49 and 51).

The differences in status which did exist between Queen Neferet and the anonymous woman in the Hathor wig are indicated visually in different ways. The queen's image is not only much larger, but was enhanced by the addition of secondary materials in the form of originally inlaid eyes.

The royal status of this larger representation is indicated by the presence of a uraeus, or cobra, set into the central part of the front of the wig, and reinforced by the fact that the queen is enthroned. The anonymous woman stands. The queen's image includes accessories in the form of bracelets and a pectoral, and the statue is inscribed. From a photograph, such differences are hardly noticeable and those imperceptible differences clearly indicate that Egyptian queens and anonymous women, might, like their male counterparts, all belong to the same elite stratum of society.

Visitors to exhibitions of ancient Egyptian art are often so overwhelmed by the size of the images they encounter as well as the hardness of the stones from which they are sculpted, that they often fail to realize just how delicate the work of accomplished craftsmen can be. The bracelets and pectoral of Neferet were created by incising pencil-thin lines into the granite. Such fine, detailed work characterizes the sculpture of the Middle Kingdom and is almost never seen in statuary from any other period, either before or after.

**Statuette of a woman
in a Hathor wig** (page 74)
**Middle Kingdom, Dynasty 12
Steatite; 7 1/2" in height
Said to be from Upper Egypt; CG 474**
Although the ancient Egyptians are
noted for the colossal scale of both
their architecture and sculpture,
their craftsmen were quite capable
of manufacturing exquisite images
on a much reduced scale, as this
statuette reveals.

In an attempt to differentiate male
from female images, the Egyptian
designers reserved the advanced left
leg for images of the striding, male
figure, whereas the female
counterpart was usually represented
as here, in a standing attitude with
both feet placed closely together.
And whereas statues of striding, male
figures generally hold folded bolts
of cloth in either one or both of their
balled fists, the hands of women are
usually empty and are depicted with
the open palms pressed against their
thighs. The anonymous woman is
shown wearing the tightly fitting
sheath, which gained currency as a
funerary garment during the course
of the Old Kingdom. Nevertheless
its style changed over time. The
configuration of the straps of the
bodice in Middle Kingdom examples,
which form a trapezoidal pattern, can
easily be distinguished from the Old
Kingdom examples where the pattern
is V-shaped.

The woman wears an elaborate wig,
the ends of which curl and rest upon
her breasts. Such a wig is often
associated with goddesses, Hathor in
particular, and could either signify
that the owner was a priestess of that
goddess, or that she wished to be
possessed of her qualities for her
aspired resurrection in the hereafter.

Statue of Pharaoh Amunemhat III
(previous page)
**Middle Kingdom, Dynasty 12
Gray granite; 34 1/4" in height
From Thebes; CG 42020**
This statue of Amunemhat III can
profitably be compared to the family
group of Ukhhotep (pages 78-79)
for it exhibits several important
similarities. There is almost no
difference in the treatment of the
physiognomic features which imbue
the faces with frowns. This appearance
is achieved by the heavy upper lids
of the eyes as well as by the down-
turned lips. Pharaoh and members of
the elite look alike because they share
in the same political outlook.
However, the difference in status
between Ukhhotep and Amunemhat
III is revealed by their costumes,
although, again, both are bare-
chested. Pharaoh is shown wearing
the nemes-headdress, fronted by
a uraeus. This accessory is a time-
honored insignia of Egyptian

pharaohs. His kilt, with its flare,
is secured to the waist by the tuck to
the right of the navel, and that detail
subtly violates the otherwise
symmetrical arrangement of the
figure. The kilt itself is decorated with
a narrow apron-like accessory, termed
a sporran, suspended from the belt.
The bottom of this sporran is
decorated with two uraei, or cobras,
which may indicate the king's divinity.
The treatment of the king's body is in
keeping with the artistic tenets of the
day, because the anatomical
tripartition of human bodies has again
been reduced to bipartition. The
upper arms have not been cut free
from the matrix of the block of stone
from which the figure was sculpted,
but remain attached to the torso by
means of negative stone, the presence
of which is clearly visible.

**Funerary stela of Nemetiemhat,
the Chief Physician,
and of Tutu, the Lector Priest
Middle Kingdom, Dynasty 11
Painted limestone; 22 3/8" in height
From Abydos; CG 20088**
The state of the paint's preservation
on this stela is remarkable, as is the
fact that the figures in the main
register are sculpted in raised relief,
whereas the figures in the lower
register are in sunk relief. Such
a combination of styles is very rare.
The main scene depicts the two
principal figures seated before a table,
with offering bearers to the right. The
offering formula here is interesting
because of the mention of a great
many deities, among which is Hekat,
the frog-goddess. *A boon which the
king grants to the god Osiris, foremost
of the Westerners, to the god Anubis,
Lord of the Necropolis, to the goddess
Hekat, to the god Khnum, and to all
of the deities who are in Abydos that
they may give the invocation offering
of bread and beer, oxen and fowl,
alabaster and cloth, and all things
good and pure on which a god lives...*
The offering formula is intended for
both Tutu, who was a lector priest,
that is one who recited the necessary
spells and religious prayers, as well
as for Nemetiemhat, whose titles are
Chief Physician, The-one-who-wields-
power-over-the-scorpion-goddess-
Selkit, and scribe. Because Selkit, the
scorpion goddess, was often
associated with magic, the fact that
Nemetiemhat bears both titles in
succession strongly suggests that this
medical practice often intersected with
the performance of religious rituals,
reinforcing the statement made earlier
about the magical aspect of ancient
Egyptian medical practice in the
periods after the Old Kingdom.

Statue Group of Ukhhotep, Hereditary Prince, Count, and Overseer of the Priests of Hathor, together with his two wives, and a daughter
Middle Kingdom, Dynasty 12
Gray granite; 11 3/4" in height
From Meir; CG 459

The incised detail which characterizes the depiction of the jewelry of Queen Neferet (pages 72-73) was used to equally good advantage in this group image of Ukhhotep, his two wives, and daughter. Ukhhotep's head is framed by a pair of wedjet-eyes, associated with the god Hor, which are meant to convey that god's protection. Each side of the round-topped slab against which the family members stand is decorated with delicately incised heraldic plants, the papyrus of Lower Egypt and the so-called sedge plant of Upper Egypt (at the spectator's right and left, respectively). The appearance of these two plants in association with the wedjet-eyes may imply that Ukhhotep had royal aspirations, despite the small scale of his monument. One recalls the predilection of members of the elite (page 70) to assume royal prerogatives in unassumingly veiled ways.

Both wives, Nebkau and Khnumhotep, wear Hathor wigs, which were very popular at this time, as well as the tightly-fitting sheath with the trapezoidal strap pattern, which is also worn by the daughter, named Nebhethenetesen. Her hair is interestingly arranged into two fanciful shaped pigtails, recalling the side lock often associated with youngsters (page 70). It is not certain which, if either, of the two women was her birth mother, but polygamy seems to have been a common occurrence in the Middle Kingdom; Hekaib (pages 84-85) also appears to have had two wives. It is interesting to note as well that all four figures are depicted in the same attitude, in which the feet are together and the palms of the hands rest on the thighs. The treatment of the anatomy of the figures deserves comment, because the high, wasp-waists of the women, accentuating their small breasts placed high on the chest, reflect an ideal of ancient Egyptian female beauty which is to be repeated throughout the history of ancient Egyptian art. Both wives, and, to a certain extent, the daughter as well seem to share the same facial features exhibited in the face of Ukhhotep. These include the heavy upper eyelids and the somewhat dour-looking, downward turn of the lips imparting a frown to the face. The same features are often encountered on the faces of certain pharaohs of the period, as a comparison with the facial features of a statue identified as Amunemhat III reveals (page 75). The explanation for this phenomenon resides in the observation that all members of the elite were, at this time, sharing in the same visual vocabulary which indicated that they subscribed to the same ideology. Furthermore, the ears of all of the figures are disproportionately large in relation to their heads, and the arms, without any indications of either the elbow joint or the wrists, lie as if inorganically glued to the sides of the bodies. Such observations should indicate that ancient Egyptian craftsmen were not primarily interested in the accurate anatomical portrayal of the human body.

**Relief from a wall of
the tomb of Mesenesen
Middle Kingdom, Dynasty 12
Limestone, with traces of paint;
32 1/2" in length
From Abydos; CG 20472**

Representations such as this are extremely important for understanding the development of ancient Egyptian art. The deceased is accorded prominence by virtue of the fact that his figure occupies the position at the spectator's left. The shape of his head is a Middle Kingdom version of what would develop into the characteristically egg-shaped head frequently employed for representations of the daughters of Akhenaton (pages 106-107). The configuration of that head is combined with the corpulence of Mesenesen's body, a convention first introduced during the Old Kingdom and continually repeated throughout the history of ancient Egyptian art. This obesity is an artistic symbol connoting elevated status. If one can excuse the pun, officials such as Mesenesen, and their directives, carried a lot of weight. The inscriptions mention almost 40 other individuals, most of whom seem to be his relatives. These include the imperfectly preserved names of his mother and father, his siblings, and children. The very mention of their names in the inscriptions on the walls of his tomb would symbolically guarantee their participation in all of the funerary ceremonies performed for, and associated with, the cult of Mesenesen. Such familial devotion is common during the Middle Kingdom. As one examines the culture of ancient Egypt more closely, one realizes that periods separated by centuries could be bridged by the craftsmen because they had a habit of repeating earlier motifs at later times. One can tentatively suggest, therefore, that many cultural features associated with the reign of Akhenaton (pages 104-106) were based on precedents established during the Middle Kingdom. These include not only the characteristic shape of the head and the corpulence, but an intense emphasis on family.

**Statue of Nebsekhut,
Seal Bearer of the King of Lower
Egypt and Chief Steward** (left)
**Middle Kingdom, Dynasty 12
Gray granite; 23" in height
From Thebes; CG 42039**

Just as the statue of Queen Neferet (pages 72-73) was a colossal version of the statuette of an anonymous lady (page 74), so too is this kneeling statue of Nebsekhut a variation of the type represented by that of Khety (right). In both, the male figure is shown kneeling on the ground with his garment stretched over his legs. Nebsekhut employs that tautness as a desk, recalling a similar use of the kilt in the statue of Nymaatsed (pages 54-55), and like him has a papyrus unrolled upon it.

The signs of age, which seem to imbue the face with portrait-like features, first appeared on images of members of the elite. Those individuals elected that mode of representation because it differed from the bland, idealizing physiognomies which had so dominated ancient Egyptian art and was traditionally employed for depictions of pharaohs. The choice was intentional, because those members of the elite wanted their images to appear to be visually very different from those of the pharaohs, whose status in society they were openly challenging. In time, the pharaohs of the Middle Kingdom, in an effort to close this visual gap, elected to be depicted in the same idiom. Such images, then, are to be regarded as manifestations of a cultural ideology, rather than as portraits of actual individuals. Although one generally assumes that the ancient Egyptians always represented themselves in the bloom of vigorous youth, members of the elite did elect to have themselves depicted as portly elders. This tradition has its roots in the Old Kingdom and continues unabated into the Ptolemaic and Roman Periods.

**Statue of Khety,
son of the lady Hathor** (right)
**Middle Kingdom, Dynasty 12
Gray granite; 35 1/2" in height
From Abydos; CG 480**

The attitude in which an individual is depicted in statuary is often a direct reflection of that individual's status in life. Here Khety is shown kneeling on the ground, implying his subservient position which is compatible with the function of the statue as reflected both by its findspot and inscription. The statue was found almost a century and a half ago in the northern cemetery at Abydos where it had been dedicated so that its owner might enjoy the benefits of an eternal communion with Osiris, god of the hereafter. The humble attitude of the

pose, and the slightly elevated head are visual manifestations of the imprecation contained in the prayer, sculpted as a single row of large, well-spaced, carefully drawn hieroglyphs. That prayer asks for: *A boon which the king grants to Osiris in order that he might bestow an invocation offering consisting of bread and beer, oxen and fowl, alabaster and linen, to the ka (spirit) of... Khety, son of the lady Hathor...* The statue was sculpted in such a way that the dimensions of the resulting figure correspond almost exactly with those of the block of stone from which it was crafted. The ancient Egyptian designers were careful in that regard and rarely, if ever, either transported or worked away large masses of stone. The symmetry of the figure is characteristically broken by the appearance of the left hand, emerging from beneath the cloak and resting, palm open, on the chest. Such heavily enveloped figures become extremely popular during the course of the Middle Kingdom and serve as a reminder that Egypt can, and still does, become very cold in winter, especially at night.

**Funerary stela of Hekaib
and his two wives** (overleaf)
**Middle Kingdom, Dynasty 12
Painted limestone; 28 3/4" in length
From Aswan; JE 36420**

Virtually all examples of ancient Egyptian relief and statuary were painted, regardless of the stone used. Some idea of the original appearance of that paint can be gained from this example, which was discovered by chance in an inclined passage of a slope just above the ruined Coptic, or Egyptian Christian, Convent of St. George on the hilly rise opposite the town of Aswan. The rectangular panel had been planed as two symmetrically arranged halves. Because primacy of place in two-dimensional representations is reserved, as one has seen, for the area to the spectator's left, the baton of office there passes in front of Hekaib's kilt, rather than behind it, as it does in his depiction on the right-hand side of the panel. For this reason, one may argue that Ketanukis, the wife shown on the left, was more important than Ibhat, the wife depicted on the right.

The concern for bilateral symmetry in this panel extends as well to the hieroglyphs across the top of the scene. In general one reads these signs by looking into the "eyes" of the birds, humans, and animals depicted. In this case, those eyes at the left-hand side are facing the center of the panel just as those on the right do. The result is four lines of text, two to each side of the panel's center. Their arrangement, therefore, corresponds to the arrangement of the two pairs of figures below. They read: *A boon which the king gives to Osiris, Lord of Busiris, Foremost of the Westerners, Lord of Abydos, and to Anubis, Who-rests-upon-his-mountain, Who-is-in-the-place- of-embalming, Who-is-the-Lord-of-the-cemetery, that they may [each] give the invocation offering consisting of bread and beer, oxen and fowl, to... Hekaib...*

This prayer, presented in a syncopated form, alludes to the offerings piled high on the table in the center of the panel. In keeping with certain artistic conventions, each of the offerings is depicted from its most characteristic point of view, and overlapping is kept to a minimum. In that way each item is distinct and easily recognizable. Although to a modern eye the offerings appear to be reaching to the sky, the ancient Egyptians would have understood the representation as a table cluttered with offerings.

THE NEW KINGDOM: DYNASTY 18

The Hypostyle, or Columned Hall, of the Temple of the God Amun at Karnak

Just as the Great Pyramids and Sphinx on the Giza Plateau are the visual symbols of the Old Kingdom, so too is the Hypostyle Hall at Karnak the icon of ancient Egypt's New Kingdom, an era of opulence and prestige ruled by men and women whose very names – Hatshepsut, Tuthmoses III, Akhenaton, Tutankhamun, Rameses – have become household words.

The hall's 134 columns, the tallest reaching heights of 75 feet, originally supported a ceiling in a most unusual way, because the architectural design was a visual expression of one of the most enduring aspects of the ancient Egyptian myth of creation.

Fundamental to all versions of that myth was the belief that creation occurred when the first rays of the sun on the first morning of the first day of creation struck the surface of a watery abyss, often depicted as a papyrus swamp, thereby dispelling the darkness and causing a primeval mound to rise in its midst, which provided the support necessary for the divine genitor to create.

Each capital of the central columns of this hall is equipped with what is termed an impost-block, a rectangular support which is much smaller in its dimensions than the diameter of the capital on which it rests. When viewed from the floor, the architraves, or horizontal beams which supported the ceiling, appeared to be suspended in space because the diameter of the column capital concealed the existence of the impost blocks supporting those architraves.

The resulting effect might well be compared to a modern theme park, because pharaoh and the elite priests would have entered a gigantic space, cloaked in darkness, and dominated by huge papyrus columns which seemed to strive to touch the heavens, visually hovering above them by virtue of the impost blocks. Then, by means of the clerestory windows placed high up on the exterior flanks of the hall, the rays of the sun at dawn would come pouring into the space, thereby replicating in a very visually perceptible way one of the basic principles of the ancient Egyptian creation myth. The temple itself was then regarded as the manifestation of the resulting primeval mound, and Amun within the genitor. The ancient Egyptians emerge, therefore, as the only people of the ancient world who purposefully designed their architectural forms to serve as metaphors rendering their fundamental religious concepts visual.

Although historians are always seeking causes for the decline and fall of ancient civilizations, the factors contributing to the end of the Middle Kingdom are currently being reevaluated. Scholars are now inclined to accept the theory, once firmly rejected, that Egypt was invaded by Asiatic peoples, whom the ancient Egyptians called "the leaders of the hill countries," a phrase which is often rendered into English as the Hyksos. Their occupation of the eastern Delta contributed to the weakening of the central administration and that in turn caused Egypt to revert to the system of local elites, each vying with one another for control of the land.

The study of the Hyksos, or Second Intermediate, Period is fraught with problems of interpretation, some of which impact profoundly upon Biblical studies. This much is certain. The Hyksos were an Asiatic people whose homeland was in Canaan. Their material culture, as revealed by excavations in the eastern Delta city of Tell al Daba (Avaris), where they seem to have been resident, is decidedly Asiatic and not Egyptian. As a result, some scholars whose speciality is ancient Egyptian language and history, as well as some Biblical archaeologists, now suggest that the events described at the end of the Book of Genesis and the beginning of the Book of Exodus may be reflections of certain aspects of the Hyksos occupation of that part of Egypt which is traditionally identified with the Land of Goshen. If their suggestions are accepted, the traditional dating of the Biblical narratives of the patriarch Joseph and the deliverance from Egypt's bondage led by Moses will have to be moved from Dynasty 19 to the period between the end of Dynasty 12 and that of the Hyksos Period.

The Hyksos, whatever their relationship with the Biblical narratives might eventually turn out to be, were firmly in control of the eastern Delta and established themselves there with virtually no military resistance whatsoever on the part of the ancient Egyptians. In the course of about half a century, the Hyksos presence spread as far south as Memphis. There is, however, one curious observation to be made about the Hyksos and that observation will pertain to all of the other foreign occupiers of ancient Egypt in subsequent epochs, be they Libyans, Persians, Macedonian Greeks, or Romans. Namely, the culture of ancient Egypt appears to have been so strong that each and every foreign occupier of that land abandoned the outward trappings of his own culture and adopted those of ancient Egypt. In other words, the Hyksos, although Asiatics, often paraded about in the costume and regalia of pharaoh and had their foreign names written in hieroglyphs as if they were Egyptian. Sociologists are at a loss to explain why such a set of circumstances should prevail, but I suspect it has a great deal to do with the ultra-conservative nature of the Egyptian elite. Indeed, recent investigations suggest that the Hyksos did nothing to dismantle the administrative structure of the land they were occupying. Rather, they seem to have enlisted the aid of certain Egyptian elite groups whose advantaged positions within society were assured in exchange for their cooperation with these foreign overlords. I know of no other ancient culture which was at once so impervious to foreign influence and simultaneously so effective in converting foreigners to its way of life and cultural expressions as ancient Egypt.

On the other hand, the Hyksos were technologically advanced. They were masters of horses harnessed to chariots and fought with a composite bow, whose power and range far exceeded that of the simple bow employed at the time by the ancient Egyptian archers. Their knowledge of metallurgy was consummate; they are said to have introduced the "shaduf", a contraption used to raise water from a lower to a higher level. These and other innovations were, in due time, taken over by the ancient Egyptians who put them to good use.

As the Hyksos state prospered in Lower Egypt, so too did the Kushites in Upper Egypt of the South. With the collapse of the Middle Kingdom, the Nubians successfully stormed the fortresses which the Egyptians had erected. They marched northward and eventually occupied Egypt proper, establishing themselves at the country's southern frontier at Aswan.

What little remained of an independent Egyptian elite withdrew to Thebes in Upper Egypt. There they viewed the events with alarm, and realized that they were in fact hemmed in on two fronts by two potentially powerful enemies. Whether the Hyksos and the Nubians ever planned an all-out two-pronged offensive against Thebes, launched from the north and south, respectively, is moot. Nevertheless, Kamoses, a ruler of Thebes, claims to have intercepted a diplomatic message allegedly dispatched from the Hyksos ruler, Apophis, to an unnamed Nubian king, in which such a strategy is apparently suggested: *Greetings to my son, the ruler of Kush... come north... be not timid... there is none who can stand against you in this part of Egypt... I will give him (the Theban pharaoh) no repose until you have arrived. And then we two shall divide up the towns of Egypt.*

The Wars of Liberation, in which the ancient Egyptians campaigned against both the Hyksos and the Nubians, ensued. The battles were fierce. The Egyptian pharaohs, by no means armchair generals, participated in the front lines. Evidence of their determination and courage on the field of battle comes in the form of the wounds inflicted to the head of the Theban pharaoh Sekenere Taaken, whose mummy is now in the Egyptian Museum in Cairo. His skull is fractured in at least three places. One of these fractures, on the top of his head, is in the form of a large, horizontal slit the configuration of which conforms to the shape of a Hyksos battle axe; an axe that was recovered from Tell al Daba was found to match this hole in his head exactly!

Some idea about the scope of these campaigns can be obtained from the vivid accounts preserved in the inscriptions of an official named Amasis, who habitually identifies himself as the son of his mother Ibana. These autobiographical texts are found on the walls of his tomb at Elkab: *When the town of Avaris (Tell al Daba) was besieged, I fought bravely on foot in his majesty's presence... when Avaris was plundered, I brought as spoils for myself from that city one man and three women.*

The success of such campaigns eventually routed the Hyksos and drove them from Egypt with the Egyptian army in hot pursuit. Amasis's autobiographical texts continue with this part of the campaign: *Then Sharuhen (a town in the Syria-Palestine region) was besieged for three years. His Majesty plundered it and I brought as spoils from it two women.*

Having successfully routed the Hyksos, the Egyptians then turned their attention to the southern reaches of their realm and directed a series of campaigns against the Nubians. Campaigns in these same theaters of operation continued into the reign of Pharaoh Ahmoses, who was related to Sekenere Taaken. Pharaoh Ahmoses first journeyed to the north where he slew "...the Mentiu of Asia (the Hyksos)," ridding Egypt of "the plague," as he termed their presence in the land. He then turned his attention to the south "...in order to crush the Nubian desert tribes... and accomplished a great slaughter among them."

Pharaoh Ahmoses died in bed after an eventful reign at the age of about sixty, widowing his wife, Ahmosesnefertari, a very remarkable woman whose career is important for an understanding of the role of women in ancient Egyptian society. Apparently of royal blood and suggested to have been either a full or a half sister of Pharaoh Ahmoses, her husband, Ahmosesnefertari seems to have ruled

The Wars of Liberation against the Hyksos in the north and the Nubians in the south are recounted by the Egyptian Amasis: "After his Majesty had slain the nomads of Asia [the Hyksos], he sailed south... to destroy the Nubian archers. His Majesty made a great slaughter of them, and I obtained as spoils two living men... I was then rewarded with gold... His Majesty journeyed north... he had conquered the southerners..."

Thebes at those times when her husband was engaged in military campaigns in distant lands. She appears to have taken it upon herself to restore many of the country's temples which had either been destroyed or neglected during the Hyksos Period. So influential had Ahmosesnefertari become during the reign of her son, Amunhotep I, the founder of Dynasty 18, that she was venerated by later generations.

More importantly, Ahmosesnefertari swapped, that is she literally traded, a minor priestly office for another called the Divine Wife of the god Amun. It is important to recall in this regard that money as such was not introduced into Egyptian society until much later. All financial transactions were effected by barter. In addition, one has to remember that property could be inherited, and accumulated wealth could be bequeathed to one's descendants. Within this economic context, then, the swapping of these clerical offices was accompanied by a large payment to Ahmosesnefertari of precious metals, articles of clothing, cosmetics and the like. By means of this same clever transaction, Ahmosesnefertari also acquired title to an estate in Western Thebes, as well as to the personnel to work it. The revenues generated from that estate contributed to the queen's wealth. The acquisition of such property by an ancient Egyptian woman was not uncommon because women could exercise rights equal to those of men regarding the acquisition and transfer of property and other wealth. As a general rule, the economic position of women in ancient Egypt was relatively better than it was for those of either ancient Greece or Rome.

The Divine Wife of the god Amun, as a mortal woman, made manifest the mythical ideal of the female regenerative forces that had to combine with those of the male principle in order to insure the maintenance and perpetuation of the cosmic powers responsible for creation, renewal, and resurrection. In terms of the cult of Amun, the Divine Wife played a significant role. She represented his consort, often identified as the goddess Mut. Their union guaranteed the harmony of the resulting creation because she alone could insure that her consort would be so content as to lay aside his redoubtable powers with which he might destroy as well as create.

Because the ancient Egyptians recognized the fundamental importance of the female principle in these theoretical religious issues, women could exercise such a degree of power during the New Kingdom that some, Hatshepsut for example, could become pharaohs in their own right, as had others earlier.

Egypt had no heir apparent when the son of Amunhotep I died prematurely. As a result the succession fell upon a member of the collateral branch of the royal family, Tuthmoses I. He married a sister of Amunhotep I, and they had two children, one of whom was the future Queen Hatshepsut (page 95). Hatshepsut then married her half-brother, fathered by her father Tuthmoses I (page 94). This man, her husband, eventually became pharaoh of Egypt and is known as Tuthmoses II. Pharaoh Tuthmoses II and his wife Hatshepsut had only one child, a daughter named Nefererure. Tuthmoses II also fathered a son with a royal concubine, and that son, Hatshepsut's step-son, was to become the future Tuthmoses III. It has been suggested, therefore, that Hatshepsut arranged for her daughter, Nefererure, to marry her stepson, Tuthmoses III.

Everything seemed to be going smoothly, despite this rather complicated family tree, until Hatshepsut's husband, Tuthmoses II, died suddenly, ostensibly from natural causes. Tuthmoses III, Hatshepsut's step-son, whom she had earlier married to her birth daughter, was a minor too young to rule in his own right. As a result, Hatshepsut, who was serving at the time as Divine Wife of the god Amun, came forward to serve as regent on behalf of her young step-son, according to at least one ancient text contemporaneous with the events: *Tuthmoses II went up to heaven and was united with the gods. His son (Tuthmoses III) took his place... the Divine Wife, Hatshepsut, dealt with the affairs of state. The Two Lands were under her administration and taxes were paid to her...*

The subsequent relationship between Hatshepsut and Tuthmoses III has been the subject of much speculation. One tradition maintains that Hatshepsut usurped the throne for herself after a joint rule with Tuthmoses III of three years or less. On the other hand, Tuthmoses III seems to have acquired several military titles during the period when he was allegedly suppressed by her.

Hatshepsut is perhaps best noted for her devotion to the state god, Amun, in whose cult she served as Divine Wife. She erected two obelisks, each of red granite, in his honor at Karnak, the one still standing in place measuring 29.5 meters in height and weighing an estimated 323 tons. These, she boasts in the accompanying inscription, were made and erected in the record time of seven months. Opposite Karnak on the West Bank of Thebes she ordered the construction of her mortuary temple at Deir al Bahari, just to the north of that of Montuhotep Nebhepetere, the founder of the Middle Kingdom. The choice was a conscious one inasmuch as Hatshepsut considered herself his successor as the present unifier of Egypt. The walls of that temple are decorated with two sequences worthy of mention. One contains a record of her trading expedition to the land of Punt, now convincingly thought to be in the modern nation state of Somalia. A recent examination of the texts accompanying these scenes indicates that her merchant marine never reached Punt, but rather put in at a more convenient entrepot closer to Egypt. The other sequence deals with her alleged divine birth as the daughter of the god Amun. These scenes are not unique to this temple but belong to a tradition of thematic cycles which are repeated on the walls of other temples erected in honor of other monarchs. A comparison of the scenes and inscriptions of the divine birth of Amunhotep III in Luxor Temple reveals that both belong to the same tradition. The death of Hatshepsut, ostensibly from natural causes, enabled Tuthmoses III (page 95) to assume his rightful position as pharaoh of Egypt. Tradition insists that one of his first official acts was the wanton destruction of the monuments of Hatshepsut, the objective of which was to demonstrate his utmost dissatisfaction with the shabby way in which she had treated him earlier.

Tuthmoses III is sometimes known as the Napoleon of Egypt for his successful military campaigns which extended Egypt's territorial possessions.

Soon thereafter, Tuthmoses III assumed a bellicose posture, and warred so continuously in the Middle East and in Nubia that he is often called the Napoleon of Egypt. He was remembered by posterity for having been one of the few pharaohs whose armies actually reached and crossed the Euphrates River in Mesopotamia. His campaigns were effective and brought the entire civilized world of the Eastern Mediterranean basin squarely into the orbit of Egypt. Everyone prospered.

Space does not allow one to consider here the accomplishments of the subsequent Tuthmoside pharaohs, save to mention in passing that Amunhotep II (pages 172-173) was remembered for his physical prowess as the sporting athletic pharaoh of Egypt, and Tuthmoses IV recorded in a stela, which still stands between the fore-paws of the Great Giza Sphinx, how he cleared the monster from the sands of the ages which had engulfed it and was awarded the throne of Egypt for his efforts.

The reign of Amunhotep III has recently been studied anew, and that scrutiny has produced some very startling data, resulting in a reassessment of his reign and the subsequent Amarna Period. In the past, scholars have suggested that Amunhotep III was so secure in his position as pharaoh that he followed his heart and married Ti, alleged to have been a commoner, out of his sheer love of the woman. That argument was based, in part, on the suggestion that Ti's name represented nothing more than a feminine ending in Egyptian grammar, the equivalent of -ess, as in governess in English. Today one recognizes that her name is really a diminutive form of Nefertari, and as such relates her to the family of Ahmosesnefertari as well as to that of the wife of Rameses II, also named Nefertari. Furthermore, his marriage to Ti has now been shown to have been prearranged by his parents because both he and his bride-to-be were too young at the time of their wedding to have voluntarily entered into marriage.

In the past the achievements of Amunhotep, son of Hapu, the architect and overseer of the royal works of Amunhotep III, have been lauded (pages 102-103). That assessment, too, has now been discarded. As the head of the elite, it was pharaoh Amunhotep III who directed the craftsmen in his employ and was responsible for the planning of all the artistic and architectural programs initiated during his reign. Amunhotep, son of Hapu, and others like him, as members of the elite, were simply co-opted to execute designs and commissions planned by pharaoh.

As striking as these recent developments may appear to be, they pale in comparison with the revolutionary ways in which the personality and reign of Amunhotep III's son and successor, Akhenaton, are being reassessed. For the traditionalists who have become accustomed to regard Akhenaton as a paragon of virtue, who instituted a religious reform aimed at creating a universal brotherhood of man living in peace and harmony via the agency of the aton, or sun disk, the following comments will be quite unsettling indeed.

The image of Amunhotep III as a statue, discovered recently in Luxor Temple (page 114), is inscribed on the rear with an important text which reveals that the cult of the aton was already in place during his reign. As a result of this document, and a host of others, one can no longer claim Akhenaton as the originator of the atonist reform (pages 104-105). The son seems merely to have been following a religious ideology already developed by the father.

Contrary to established belief, it was Amunhotep III, rather than his son Akhenaton, who was the true instigator of the cult of the aton. Equally, Akhenaton was not as pacifistic, nor the Amarna Period as monotheistic, as received wisdom would suggest.

The relationships between the religion of the aton and that of the Hebrews has come under attack inasmuch as some progressive scholars would now prefer to site the Egyptian background of the Old Testament narratives of Genesis and Exodus in the Middle Kingdom – Hyksos Period. Furthermore, the perceived monotheistic characteristics of the Amarna Period's religion have now been called into question insofar as the religious tenets of atonism do not satisfy the rigorous requirements of monotheism. The earlier suggestion that Akhenaton was a pacifist, ignoring the collapse and plight of his Asiatic allies in favor of devoting himself exclusively to the practice of his religion, cannot be maintained. Several contemporary documents dwell on his military campaigns, particularly those which were waged in his name against the Nubians.

The final chapter of the history of Akhenaton and of the Amarna Period has yet to be written, but one thing is certain. The Akhenaton of popular tradition, the Akhenaton who has been so lionized in novels and in Hollywood movies, the Akhenaton who has been hailed as a man of peace, is a figment of the imagination. No humanitarian would ever suffer his subjects to stand in the blazing hot Egyptian sun to worship, while he and his family were afforded the protection of shaded pavilions. Look at the art of the Amarna Period. Never before and never after have there been so many scenes of row upon row of groveling, bowing, obsequious courtiers.

From the vantage of this essay, Akhenaton, and perhaps his father, were apparently upset with the direction into which some members of the elite were

The images of Amunhotep III and Akhenaton (pages 104-105 and 114) **share distinctive characteristics which differ significantly from those of the preceding Tuthmoside pharaohs, emphasizing their promotion of the cult of the aton at the expense of their predecessors' devotion to the cult of Amun.**

headed. In my view, the struggles between Hatshepsut and Tuthmoses III are better regarded as the struggles between competing branches of the elite. Remember in this regard that Hatshepsut came from a collateral branch of the royal family, whose family members were not in line for the succession to the throne. Her apparently unilateral usurpation of power and subsequent relegation of Tuthmoses III may be regarded as the triumph of one sector of the elite over that of another. Her devotion to Amun cannot be overlooked. The respective positions, then, of the supporters of Hatshepsut and Tuthmoses III were reversed with the ascendancy of the latter. Members of the elite were very pragmatic, as one has seen during the Hyksos occupation of the land. This may account for how some officials managed to stay in the good graces of several successive pharaohs during these events.

One wonders, then, whether the purposeful promotion of the cult of the aton in the reign of Amunhotep III was an effort on the part of that monarch to distance himself from an elite which, from the time of Hatshepsut, had aligned itself with the cult of Amun. The decision taken by Akhenaton to move the capital from Thebes to Amarna has been regarded as an attempt to break the power of the Amun priesthood. In this light it appears only natural that Akhenaton, having moved to Amarna, would appoint new men to positions of responsibility. He was attempting to create a new elite, one which would remain loyal to him and which would act as a counter-balance to the elite attached to the cult of Amun.

This suggestion is not as far-fetched as it at first appears when one considers the following events. Might the estrangement of Nefertiti (pages 104-105) from Akhenaton at Amarna not signal her realization that her husband's clique was about to be eclipsed? The bloodless coup which resulted in the changing of Tutankhaton's name to Tutankhamun and the almost instantaneous return of the capital of Egypt to Thebes speaks volumes about the strength and perseverance of the elite tied to the cult of Amun and fostered by Hatshepsut, which opposed the reforms of Amunhotep III and Akhenaton. In my view, the condemnation of the memory of Hatshepsut, the erasures of the name of Amun, and later those of Akhenaton and of the aton, have to be regarded as interrelated, causal events. The vehemence with which pharaoh Horemheb appears to have torched the aton sanctuary of the gem pa aton at Karnak must be taken into consideration with his unctuous official decrees about how he returned the land to orthodoxy. By such deeds and words Horemheb aligns himself squarely with the elite faction supporting Amun. And because he adopts Rameses I as his son and successor, the pharaohs of Dynasty 19, as we will see in the next chapter, also continue to persecute the memory of Akhenaton while acknowledging the Theban elite linked to Amun.

**Head of a pharaoh,
perhaps Tuthmoses I
New Kingdom, Dynasty 18
Painted sandstone
47 1/4" in height
From Thebes; CG 42051**

Because images of pharaohs and members of the elite are visual expressions of ideology rather than representations of specific individuals, it is very difficult at times to suggest an identification for an Egyptian image, such as this head, when it lacks an accompanying inscription. Nevertheless, a tentative identification can be suggested because specific facial types were designed at particular times during the course of Egypt's history to serve as visual expressions of that epoch's prevailing ideology. The specific features of this head include the round, rather than oval, configuration of the face, and the large, hieroglyphic eyes, both framed with cosmetic lines and crowned by thick, sickle-shaped eyebrows. In profile, the nose, which is not damaged, is very aquiline, characterized by a thin bridge terminating in non-flaring nostrils. The thin lips are drawn up into a faint smile. These physiognomic features are typical of images of the Tuthmoside pharaohs of early Dynasty 18. To that conclusion may be added the observation that this head was found in the vicinity of the Fourth Pylon, or Gateway, within Karnak, which was erected under Tuthmoses I, as its accompanying inscriptions indicate. The cumulative force of this evidence suggests that this head is a representation of Tuthmoses I himself.

**Statue of a pharaoh, perhaps
Hatshepsut, reinscribed
by Tuthmoses III, striding**
(detail, page 98)
**New Kingdom, Dynasty 18
Rose granite; 70 7/8" in height
From Abydos; CG 594**

The attitude of the pharaoh represented in this statue is another example of the remarkable continuity which characterizes ancient Egyptian art; it appears to be a clone of the type used for a representation of pharaoh Amunemhat III (page 75) of the Middle Kingdom, created several centuries before. There can be no doubt that this statue is indebted to the tradition from which the earlier one emerged and both statues may, therefore, be regarded as visual expressions of kingship.

There are, however, slight variations which a modern may overlook, but which were important visual clues for those members of the ancient Egyptian elite who were taught how to understand them. The faces differ. The face of this pharaoh is characterized by features associated with the Tuthmoside rulers of early Dynasty 18 (left), and thereby avoids the signs of age manifest in the Middle Kingdom example. The accessories include a false beard, attached to the chin by means of a strap which passes along the cheeks and secures it in place. Such a beard symbolically imbues the image with power and virility. The bottom of the sporran is decorated with a row of teardrop-shaped pendants, which are lacking in the earlier example. These details are intentional and indicate that, whereas both images are royal, they are possessed of somewhat different ideological significance. The belt of this statue bears a buckle in the form of a cartouche, or royal ring, which is nothing more than the hieroglyph for a kind of cowboy's rope lasso, used to enclose those signs which spell the name of pharaoh, because the hieroglyphs do not have the modern equivalent of punctuation or capitalization. The signs within this cartouche spell the name "Tuthmoses," and confirm one's initial suspicion, based on the features of the face, that a Tuthmoside pharaoh is indeed represented. Traditionally pharaohs had five names, and since there were four pharaohs of Dynasty 18 who shared in the name "Tuthmoses," it is difficult to determine which of the four is here intended, inasmuch as no other names or titles are inscribed on this statue. It is tempting, nevertheless, to identify this statue as a representation of Tuthmoses III, the warrior pharaoh of Dynasty 18.

On the other hand, a careful examination of the way the hieroglyphs have been cut into the belt suggest that both the cartouche and the signs it contains are a later addition. These elements are less deeply cut into the stone than are the lines of the kilt's pleats and the decoration on the sporran. If this theory is accepted, it can be suggested that the statue originally represented Hatshepsut, whose memory Tuthmoses III attempted to erase by destroying some of her monuments and appropriating others for his own use. By taking over one of her statues, Tuthmoses III is claiming that he is the rightful ruler of the land. That Hatshepsut should be depicted as a man with a bare chest should come as no surprise because, as has been established, ancient Egyptian art is symbolic, not representational. Although women could become pharaohs and rule in their own right, the visual vocabulary, available to the elite, by which concepts of kingship were made manifest in art were couched in male, not female, motifs.

**Statue of the Lioness-Goddess
Sekhmet, enthroned**
(details, pages 97 and 99)
**New Kingdom, Dynasty 18
Gray granite; 78 3/4" in height
From Thebes; CG 39063**
Although the destructive nature of Sekhmet has been suggested earlier (pages 68-69), no monument better reveals just how potentially savage the unbridled force of that goddess could be in the eyes of the ancient Egyptians than the group of statues to which this example originally belonged. Whereas there is disagreement among scholars about the location of the temple in which this group originally stood, all scholars agree that the temple was located somewhere in Thebes and that the group originally consisted of 730 individual statues of Sekhmet, some enthroned as here, others standing. The reason there were so many statues of this goddess was due to her power, which, if left unchecked, could be unleashed to the detriment of Egypt and pharaoh himself. As a result, Sekhmet could be appeased only by performing specific rituals in succession before each of her statues twice a day, hence the total number of the group, which represents twice the number of days in the ancient Egyptian year.
In keeping with the design tenets of ancient Egyptian art, the composite images harmoniously combine the leonine head to the body of a woman, the juncture of which is masked not only by the mane but also by the broad collar and lappets of the wig which fall over each breast (right). The cosmic nature of the goddess is suggested by the presence of the sun disk on her head, fronted by the uraeus, emblem of her strength. The symmetry of the pose is again violated, this time by the sign of life, the ankh, which she holds on her thigh with her left hand (page 99). This group of statues was commissioned by Amunhotep III, under whose reign more animal sculptures were created than during the reign of any other monarch. The inscriptions in the two columns on the front of the throne name him: *The good god, the lord of action, Nebmaatre* [one of Amunhotep's five names], *beloved of Sekhmet, the mistress of dread, who gives life, eternally. The son of the god Re of his own body, Amunhotep, ruler at Thebes, beloved of Sekhmet, the mistress of dread, who gives life, eternally.* These inscriptions clearly indicate that the goddess, who brings fear to the hearts of the Egyptians, is capable of granting them life as well, provided her cultic requirements are satisfied on a twice daily basis.

**Bust of the pharaoh Akhenaton
New Kingdom, Dynasty 18
Sandstone; 52" in height
From Thebes; JE 15899/4**
Images of pharaoh Akhenaton, created early in his reign, as here, are characterized by facial features which appear to be so radically different from anything ever created before in ancient Egypt that some scholars have attempted to use those features as the basis of diagnosing alleged physiological problems from which that pharaoh may have suffered. The futility of such lines of investigation is immediately evident when one acknowledges that ancient Egyptian art was symbolic rather than representational.

Many of the features inherent in the face of such statues of Akhenaton were already developed for the depiction of his father, Amunhotep III, and the elite members of that court (pages 100 and 103). These include the small, almond-shaped eyes set obliquely into the head, as well as the prominence given to the cheekbones. The long, protruding chin appears already in its initial form in representations contemporary with Amunhotep III (page 100). That the representation under discussion is a symbol of kingship is clear because of the presence of the nemes-headdress and its uraeus. This particular image of Akhenaton is one of only four known examples among the many excavated at Thebes which depict the pharaoh with the four feathers associated with Shu, who was linked with the brilliant light, or illumination, which issued forth from the aton.

The Valley of The Kings

Already a source of wonder in Classical times when scores of visitors entered many of the tombs of the pharaohs, which had anciently been plundered, and left graffiti in Greek on their walls as proof of their visits, these silent sepulchers, cut deep into the limestone hills of Thebes, still fascinate the general public and attract the attention of archaeologists. Some of these tombs have only recently been re-entered, and the academic consensus maintains that there may yet be more tombs in the Valley awaiting discovery.

The very name, Valley of the Kings, is itself a misnomer, because queens, such as Hatshepsut, parents of queens, and even highly placed members of the elite have been buried here in tombs which have been identified. Almost all of these are decorated with religious scenes accompanied by arcane inscriptions of the kind which first appeared in Dynasty 5 on the walls of the Pyramid of Unas at Sakkara . Many symbolically recount the journey of the deceased pharaoh through the netherworld on his way to spiritual rebirth in the aspired Egyptian hereafter. In some, pharaoh is compared to the sun, whose nocturnal journey along the "night Nile" would ultimately end with its rising at dawn, metaphorically suggesting the king's rebirth as well.

It is known that a special police detachment was assigned to patrol the heights of these cliffs into which the sepulchers were cut as a deterrent against theft. The entrances to the tombs were themselves covered over with stones and sand so that a casual visitor might be fooled into thinking that they were nothing more than natural rock slides.

Despite these precautions, many of the tombs were plundered in ancient times. Some, such as that of Tutankhamun, still retained the lion's share of their furnishings when explored by archaeologists. It is, however, a gross error to think that the treasure of Tutankhamun's tomb is unique. The French scholar Pierre Montet discovered royal tombs, equally well-appointed and flowing with gold and silver objects, at Tanis in the Nile Delta (pages 178-187), but that discovery was overshadowed by the outbreak of World War II. The imagination runs wild, therefore, when one considers that the locations of the tombs of the pharaohs of Dynasties 26, 28, 29, and 30, as well as that of Alexander the Great, Cleopatra the Great, and the Ptolemies have yet to be identified. Who knows what treasures still lurk within those sepulchers, if fortune has smiled upon their owners and they remain intact, awaiting the application of an Egyptologist's trowel!

Statue of a deity enthroned, inscribed for "Rameses, Beloved of Isis"
New Kingdom, Dynasty 18
Reinscribed in Dynasty 19
Gray granite; 71" in height
From Sheikh Abada (Antinoe)
JE 39063

As has been noted, inscriptions on statues are no guarantee either of the original commissioner of the work (page 95), or of its initial location. This statue is another example of that phenomenon. The two short texts in hieroglyphs on the base at either side of the feet are clear: *The good god, Wesermaatre Septenre* (one of the five names of Rameses II), *beloved of Isis. The son of the sun god, Re, Rameses [II], beloved of Isis.* On the face value of this inscription, the statue should be assigned to Dynasty 19 and understood as a commission ordered by Rameses II. On the other hand, a closer examination of the statue, particularly the sides of the throne, reveal very uneven surfaces which indicate that the original inscriptions may have been intentionally chiseled off.

The cartouches of Rameses II would have then been added on each side of the feet. This suggestion is supported by the face of the deity, which represents a departure from the habitual depiction of the Tuthmoside pharaohs. The almond-shaped eyes are set into the head at a more oblique angle; there is a greater interest in the cheekbones, and the thin lips are pursed into a distinctive smile. These characteristics are encountered on images which are uniformly inscribed with the names and titles of Amunhotep III and those members of the elite who served under him.

There is, therefore, every good reason to suggest that this statue was crafted during the reign of Amunhotep III and was later usurped by Rameses II who reinscribed it in his own honor. The identify of the deity depicted is problematic, because the only distinctive attribute, the was-scepter, was commonly shared by several deities. Moreover, the gender of the deity is in question. To modern sensibilities the figure appears to be that of a god, and yet the Rameside inscription clearly associates the figure with the goddess Isis. Once again, the ancient Egyptian craftsmen have demonstrated that their art is symbolic, not representational.

Statue of the official Amunhotep, son of Hapu
New Kingdom, Dynasty 18
Gray granite; 39 1/2" in height
From Thebes; CG 551

The pose of this statue is a time-honored one, usually reserved for pharaohs (pages 75 and 95), but here it has been appropriated by Amunhotep, son of Hapu, whose connections with his sovereign, Amunhotep III, were very close. His image does, however, differ significantly from that of the pharaoh, notably through the omission of certain details, reserved for royal depictions. These include the nemes-headdress with its accompanying uraeus, which has here been replaced with an elaborately curled wig. And the kilt, instead of the sporran associated with royal images, reveals in its place a single column of hieroglyphs (left), containing part of the offering formula: *All that which comes forth upon the offering table of the god Khonsu in* [Thebes?]...

A closer look at the inscription reveals that the last few hieroglyphs, before the final sign of an owl, have been cut away. This is determined by the level of the stone, which, in this area, is lower than that above and below it. Having chiseled that section off, the stone was then recut with hieroglyphs spelling the name of the god, Khonsu. The unavoidable conclusion is, therefore, that the removed hieroglyphs spelled the name of the god Amun and were removed by the agents of Akhenaton when he proscribed that god as part of his continuing promotion of the cult of the aton.

The addition of the name of the god Khonsu may have occurred at any subsequent period, because one knows that the reputation of

Amunhotep, son of Hapu, was so great that he was continually invoked by later generations of Egyptians, right through to the Ptolemaic Period, as an intercessor on their behalf with the gods. Many of his statues were still standing in Thebes centuries after his death, their surfaces having been worn away because they were constantly touched during those invocations by the faithful.

This particular statue is art historically important because it demonstrates the non-representational nature of ancient Egyptian art. To a modern, the face of Amunhotep, son of Hapu, appears here to represent a vigorous male in the prime of life. As such, his face contrasts with the corpulence of his torso, for it is not the face of an obese person. However, the corpulence of the torso is not a realistic depiction of obesity, but rather the symbolic representation of rank. Men like Amunhotep, son of Hapu, as well as Mesenesen (pages 80-81), are depicted this way as a visual sign that they have worked their way up the bureaucratic ladder, as Seankhenptah (page 58) had done before them. Corpulence in these instances is to be regarded, therefore, as an artistic convention emblematic of the individual's elevated status within the ranks of the elite.

**Representation of Pharaoh
Akhenaton, his queen Nefertiti,
and two of their daughters**
(pages 104-105,detail)
**New Kingdom, Dynasty 18
Limestone; 20 3/4" in height
Findspot not known; 10/11/26/4**
The original function of this
interesting representation is a matter
of speculation, because its findspot
has not been recorded. It may have
been part of a relief, decorating the
wall of a shrine or building, or,
as seems more likely, a stela, or
commemorative stone. In keeping
with ancient Egyptian artistic
conventions whereby the largest
figures in any composition are the
most important, the image of
Akhenaton towers over those of the
members of his family (not shown).
Nevertheless, the height of Nefertiti's
crown, due to the double plumes,
effectively renders her the tallest
figure in the scene, thereby
suggesting her importance as well.
One must remember that the
monuments excavated at eastern
Karnak, which are dated to the early
part of her husband's reign, depict
Nefertiti in a very prominent, if not
to say, dominant role.

**Head of a daughter
of Pharaoh Akhenaton
New Kingdom, Dynasty 18
Quartzite; 4 1/4" in height
From Amarna; JE 65040**
Despite the recent revisionist
approach to the reign and ideology
of Akhenaton (page 93), earlier
observations which remarked on the
strong familial ties which he
apparently had with the members
of his family, at least initially, remain
intact. The sheer number of
representations, which have survived,
depicting Akhenaton together with
his family members, or of his family
members by themselves, are without
precedent in the entire history
of Egyptian art. Why this should
be remains a matter of speculation,
although it has been suggested
already that the impetus for such
depictions may have originated during
the course of the Middle Kingdom
(pages 70 and 80-81).
This head, which is not inscribed,
is typical of the way in which the
daughters of Akhenaton were
depicted.It is characterized by a very
elongated skull, which some
commentators have unsuccessfully
attempted to link to the practice
of binding, while others suggest that
such images represent a physical
deformity, hydrocephalus being the
affliction most frequently suggested.

However, the elongated, egg-shaped
skull has antecedents in the Middle
Kingdom; a similar form was
employed in the representation of
Mesenesen, whose corpulence (page
80) likewise prefigures that
encountered for images of this period
as well. As was the case with the
images of Akhenaton himself, this
depiction of his daughter is symbolic,
for it distances the members of the
royal family from all others; it is a
manifestation of the family's religious
beliefs, which were intended to
distinguish its adherents from the
worshippers of ancient Egypt's
traditional deities.

THE DISCOVERY OF THE LUXOR CACHETTE

Previous page
**View of the Sun Court of
Amunhotep III in Luxor temple,
site of the discovery of
the Luxor Cachette**
Ever since the time of Napoleon's
epoch-making expedition to Egypt
in 1798, native Egyptians, students,
scholars, and tourists of all
descriptions have walked over every
inch of this unpaved court, unaware
of the treasures which lay inches
beneath its surface. Those treasures,
coming from what is now termed the
Luxor Cachette, were accidentally
discovered in the northwest corner of
this open court on January 22, 1989.

Just about everywhere one goes in Egypt today, one sees evidence of how ground water, because of the increased height of the water table, penetrates via capillary action into the stones of the monuments, both ancient and modern alike. As this water passes from the earth to those monuments it carries minerals in solution. Working its way to the surfaces of the blocks of stone, the water eventually evaporates, but the composition and nature of the minerals contained in solution are not so readily dissipated. They are left behind, forming crystals just beneath the surface of the stones which increase in size until, like so many miniature bombs, they erupt causing the surface of the block of stone, and the decoration on it, to spall away from the wall. The problem is both serious and endemic, particularly at Luxor Temple.

As a result, the Egyptian antiquities authority conducts a series of routine inspections, the objective of which is to gauge the height of the water table. Early in January, 1989, an inspector, as the antiquities officials on archaeological sites are called, who had just joined the service, was directed to sign for the probe by which those tests were conducted and proceed with a workman to Luxor Temple, where he was to collect the data necessary for determining the height of the water table. Realizing that the Sun Court of Amunhotep III is a popular area in which tourists like to rest, he discreetly walked over to the northwest corner, selected a suitable spot on the ground, and attempted to drive in his probe. The probe met with resistance. He removed the instrument, moved a bit to one side, and shoved it in once more. Again, he experienced the same result. When the third attempt to drive the probe into the soil in this part of Luxor Temple was likewise foiled, the perplexed inspector instructed the workman to assist him in digging up the ground so as to determine the nature of the obstruction. Not equipped to conduct a proper excavation, the inspector and his workman soon uncovered a rectangular slab of diorite which was apparently uninscribed. They hurriedly recovered this stone, and dutifully reported the incident to their superiors. The next day, a properly constituted team returned to the site and began to dig where the young inspector indicated. What they uncovered turned out to be a base into which two statues were originally placed (page 115). It had been buried face down in the earth, so that the inspector and his workman encountered its bottom surface. Imagine, then, the luck involved when repeated attempts to probe the soil successively hit one and the same object. What are the random chances of that happening at all?

When the base was removed, the archaeological trench was enlarged. Soon several statues, in complete states of preservation, were discovered. These included images of the pharaoh Horemheb and of the god Atum (page 115), which fit perfectly into the base initially discovered, as well as images of two enthroned goddesses, inscribed respectively for Hathor (page 112) and Eunet (page 113). But the biggest surprise of all was the way in which these objects had been intentionally interred as if to form a box of protection around a further discovery – an eight foot tall statue of Amunhotep III (page 114)! The circumstances contributing to this ritual interment of these statues is perhaps to be attributed to the presence of the Roman garrison which was responsible for closing down Luxor Temple (pages 210-211). In an effort to save these statues from the hands of the Romans, certain members of the Egyptian elite elected to bury them, very carefully indeed, in the hope of returning after the Roman threat had passed and recover them.

As the archaeological trench was progressively enlarged in order to remove the statue of Amunhotep III, at first no other statues were found. The trench perforce had to be dug even deeper, in order to accommodate the removal of

**Statue of the Goddess Hathor,
enthroned** (page 112)
New Kingdom, Dynasty 18
Diorite; 60 1/8" in height
Luxor Museum
This image of the goddess Hathor
is virtually identical to that of Eunet
(page 113). Both deities are
represented enthroned; they hold
the sign of life, the ankh, on their
thigh with the right hand, and
wear identical costumes. Hathor
is distinguished from Eunet by her
traditional attribute, a platform,
termed a modius, which supports the
sun disk and cow's horns. The two
columns of hieroglyphs conform, in
their contents, to those found on the
statue of Sekhmet (page 96), which
also name Amunhotep III: *The good
god, Nebmaatre, beloved of Hathor
in Ipetreset, who grants life. Son of the
sun god, Re, Amunhotep, ruler in
Thebes, beloved of Hathor in Ipetreset.*
Ipetreset is one of the ancient
Egyptian names for Luxor Temple.

**Statue of the Goddess Eunet,
enthroned** (page 113)
New Kingdom, Dynasty 18
Gray granite; 57 1/4" in height
Luxor Museum
This statue of Eunet, inscribed for
Amunhotep III, is remarkable because
it is the only known representation
of this goddess, whose existence is
known from inscriptions, as a statue.
She is depicted wearing a tightly-
fitting sheath, the only indication
of which is the appearance of the hem
at the level of the ankles. Her only
attribute is the sign of life, the ankh,
which she holds to her lap in her right
hand. The inscriptions on the sides
of her throne are identical to those
found on the statue of Hathor (page
112), with the single exception that
here the name of Hathor has been
substituted for that of Eunet.

that statue. Then suddenly, after an interval of a certain distance, more statues began to appear.

The random nature in which these additional statues were found was expected because of the ancient Egyptian practice of periodically clearing out their temples. After time, the number of statues dedicated in any given temple became so great that there was little room for additional sculpture in the precinct. A house-cleaning was ordered, but because the previously dedicated statues were sacred to the deities, they could not be discarded as refuse. The expedient was then found by which a hole, large enough to accommodate all of the statues, was dug within the temple. Once the statues had been tossed into it, the hole was refilled. A deposit, similar to this one at Luxor Temple, was also discovered at Karnak and was excavated between 1903-1906. The Karnak deposit contained approximately 750 stone statues and another 1700 of bronze. The Luxor deposit, however, yielded fewer than 30 statues before work had to stop because the ground water was rapidly filling the excavation trench. The water then began to erode away the walls of the trench, which threatened the stability of the columns in that part of the Sun Court. Work stopped, and the trench was then filled. Today, the colonnade of the Sun Court of Luxor Temple is being dismantled in order to reconstruct it in a more stabilized way. That reconstruction may be accompanied by further excavation of the Cachette – a word taken from the French who originally directed the excavations of the Karnak deposit – which may result in the discovery of even more statues.

**Representation of Pharaoh
Amunhotep III as a statue on a sledge
New Kingdom, Dynasty 18
Quartzite; 98" in height
Luxor Museum**

Of all of the statues recovered to date from the Luxor Cachette, none has caused as much excitement as this one, both as a result of its perceived quality and its fantastic state of preservation. The representation is important for other reasons as well. To begin with, the image is an ancient Egyptian representation of the king as a statue, an observation supported by the fact that the image is depicted resting on a sledge. Secondly, the rough surfaces on the chest and forearms represent an original abrading of the surfaces. This was to anchor the fixative which was used to hold the now missing gold leaf employed to indicate the jewelry worn by the statue. In addition to the jewelry, the statue's accessories include a false beard, the double crown fronted by a uraeus, an elaborately pleated kilt, and sandals. The statue must have been visible during the Amarna Period, because each occurrence of the name Amun in the cartouches of Amunhotep III have been intentionally erased.

This is all the more remarkable when one considers the contents of the inscriptions on the back pillar. There one of Amunhotep's epithets reads: *...the aton who illuminates the Two Lands, the uraeus who causes the Twin River Banks [Egypt] to be illuminated...* Inscriptions such as this, safely dated to the reign of Amunhotep III and clearly linking him to the aton, demonstrate beyond any doubt that he, rather than his son, Akhenaton, was the one initially responsible for introducing and promoting that religious movement (pages 92-93). It is doubtless for this reason that only those hieroglyphs used in the writing of the name Amun were chiseled out of the statue. The rest remained untouched, because of its close associations with the aton itself.

**Statue Group of Horemheb
kneeling in adoration before
the God Atum, enthroned
New Kingdom, Dynasty 18
Diorite; 59 1/2" in length
Luxor Museum**

The effects of the soil upon the surfaces of these two statues accounts for their perceived different colors. Horemheb, in a plain kilt, wearing as accessories only the nemes-headdress fronted by a uraeus and false beard, kneels before his god, proffering nu-pots, which are traditionally associated with liquid libations. The god Atum, guarantor of kingship, is dressed in a similarly unadorned kilt, but wears the Double Crown and holds the sign of life on his thigh with his left hand. The sides of his throne are decorated with representations of fecundity figures shown in the act of uniting, literally tying together with a square knot, the Two Lands, represented by their respective heraldic plants (page 79). These motifs, which visually associate Atum with kingship, are reinforced by the statement made by the inscriptions on the back pillar: *A prayer offered by the god Atum, the Lord of the Two Lands, the Heliopolitan: Oh my beloved son, the sovereign of the Two Lands, Djeserkheperure Setepenre Hekamaat, the son of the sun god, Re, Horemheb, beloved of Amun, I have established you eternally as the pharaoh of the Two Lands in recognition of the beautiful, enduring, and lasting monuments which you have caused to be erected in my honor.*

The absence of detail, such as the pleating on the kilts, may be due to the disappearance of the paint which originally covered both figures. When discovered, minute traces of blue and yellow pigment were found on the throne, but they soon vanished because of their unstable condition caused by the soil in which they had for so long been buried.

THE NEW KINGDOM: DYNASTIES 19-20

One of the five names of Rameses II was pronounced in ancient times something like Wesermaatre in English, which the Greeks who visited Egypt heard as Ozymandias. Western tradition has rather romantically clung to that sobriquet for Rameses II, and this has led to some rather unexpected, and unfortunate results. The enormous temple complex, which was erected so that the cult of Rameses II might be celebrated after his death, was decorated with statues, some of which were of colossal scale. One such statue still remains here in the Rameseum, in a somewhat damaged state. It originally stood almost 60 feet in height in front of the Second Pylon, or gateway, of the temple, and weighed an estimated 1,000 tons. Perhaps as a result of an earthquake or human depredation, the statue fell with its head landing inside the courtyard behind the pylon, where it still rests. This monumental statue, often termed the colossal Ozymandias, has been romantically linked with a sonnet of the same name written by the English poet P. B. Shelley. Most visitors to the site still link the poem to this statue. But Shelley never actually saw this statue in person. *I met a traveller from an antique land who said...* The statue which the traveller then describes has been shown to be a colossal bust acquired by the British Museum in 1818, a year before Shelly wrote his sonnet. The poet used that bust as his source of inspiration for the sonnet, and as a result of his familiarity with the bust created a verbal image *...two vast and trunkless legs of stone ...a shattered visage...* which bears absolutely no relationship to the physical state of the Rameseum colossus because the *...frown and wrinkled lip, and sneer of cold command* do not exist on the face of the colossus! Its facial features are almost entirely obliterated. Moreover, anyone who visits the Rameseum today or looks at images or photographs of the site from the last century soon realizes that *the lone and level sands* do not *stretch far away.* The suggestion that the Egyptological community should attempt to restore the Rameseum colossus has been met with a cry of outrage in less enlightened quarters, the loudest protests coming from individuals who still cling rather romantically to a tradition linking Shelley's poem with the statue, an association that has no basis in fact.

The accession to the throne of Rameses I marks a significant turning point in the history of Egypt. Born into a military family of long standing with roots in the eastern Delta, Rameses I was already advanced in age when he became pharaoh of Egypt. He realized that the Theban elite, centered around the cult of Amun at Karnak, was a powerful force with which to contend. In order to gain their acceptance, he initiated a series of building programs at Karnak. He even modelled the decoration of his tomb in the Valley of the Kings (page 101) on that of his adoptive father, Horemheb. Satisfied that he had reached an accommodation with that faction, Rameses I realized that the security of Egypt was being threatened by hostile forces from abroad. His brief reign of about two years precluded his aggressive participation in campaigns against these new enemies, but such military encounters were to become hallmarks of Egypt's foreign policy during the course of Dynasties 19 and 20.

Sety I, his son and successor, continued to favor the Theban elite of the god Amun, and took active steps to distance himself from the dissident faction of both Hatshepsut and Akhenaton. To that end, he ordered his scribes to compile a Kings' List, that is a chronological arrangement of all of the "acceptable" pharaohs of Egypt. The list, sculpted on to the walls of the Temple of Sety I at Abydos, to the north of Thebes, contains the names of sixty-seven pharaohs. It begins with Menes, whom historians now maintain was a legendary pharaoh intentionally created just for such purposes by these scribes, and ends with Sety I himself. It is interesting to observe how the name of Hatshepsut, as well as of all of those of the Amarna pharaohs, including not only Akhenaton but also Tutankhamun, have been omitted by this very selective editing of Egypt's history. It is precisely because of such tampering with the historical evidence by the ancient Egyptians themselves that many epochs of Egypt's history, particularly the Amarna Period, are so imperfectly understood today.

Having attempted to eradicate the memory of the divisive pharaohs of Dynasty 18 from his official annals, Sety I was compelled to deal with Egypt's foreign foes. Foremost among them were apparently groups of marauding tribes which threatened the allies of Egypt in the region. *May the king [of Egypt], my lord, the sun of the sky... give me help... lest the Apiru destroy us* implores one of the petty princes of the area, firmly in the Egyptian camp. Adding to the apparent confusion was the presence of the Hittites.

The Hittites, an Indo-European group of people, had settled in the heartland of what is now the modern nation state of Turkey and there established a capital, Bogazkoy (Hattusa), not far from Ankara. In time, Hittite interests inclined them to move southward into the Syria-Palestine area, a region which, during Dynasty 18, was nominally under the control of the Egyptians. Hittite penetration into that area is not necessarily to be regarded as a military challenge against Egypt. *...the request that your father [the previous pharaoh of Egypt] made, saying, 'Let us establish only the most friendly relations between us,' did I indeed refuse?*, asks Suppiluliumas, the king of the Hittites, of an unnamed pharaoh of the Amarna Period.

Against this background, one momentous episode in Egyptian history stands out, but its satisfactory resolution is shrouded in mystery. An unnamed Egyptian queen, married to an unspecified pharaoh of the Amarna Period who had recently died, wrote as a widow to the same Suppiluliumas requesting the hand of one of his sons in marriage. Prince Zennanza, his son, was sent to Egypt, but disappeared mysteriously en route. Some historians claim the Egyptian widow was Ankhenesamun, the eldest daughter of Akhenaton, whereas others claim the death of Zennanza was ordered by Horemheb.

Whatever the resolution of this great plot for a murder mystery might be, Hittite-Egyptian relations were strained, and military hostilities between these two super-powers would escalate during the course of Dynasty 19. The ensuing tug-of-war between the Hittites and the Egyptians for the hegemony of Syria resulted in a pragmatic truce in the form of a treaty between Sety I and Muwatallis, the new Hittite king. Nevertheless, the cessation of hostilities was merely a ruse because both sides used the ensuing interval of alleged peace to rearm and plan renewed military campaigns.

Hostilities erupted during the reign of Rameses II, the son and successor of Sety I, when the Egyptian armies marched north into Syria and engaged the forces of the Hittites at the city of Kadesh, today Tell Nebi Mend, on the Orontes River, not far from the Syrian city of Homs. The account of the battle contained all of the elements of epic: spies planted by the Hittites whose objective was to be captured by the Egyptians in order to give false intelligence; a tactical error on the part of Rameses II which distanced him from most of his forces; the eleventh hour arrival of those forces; and so forth. Rameses II claimed victory, and his official account of the battle and its outcome was recorded no less than thirteen times throughout the length and breadth of Egypt. Such bombast is, of course, now tempered by the realization that the outcome of the Battle of Kadesh, as recorded in contemporary Hittite documents, was a draw.

Rameses II was compelled to return to the region as the hostilities continued, but another major military clash was averted by a palace coup within the land of the Hittites. Uri-teshub, an illegitimate son of Muwatallis, against whom Rameses II fought at Kadesh, assumed the throne, ousting his uncle Hattusilis III. In the ensuing family feud, Hattusilis III in turn ousted Uri-teshub, who, after several vicissitudes, turned up at the Egyptian court of Rameses II seeking refuge. Diplomacy, rather than weapons, now prevailed, and the situation was resolved three years later when Rameses II and his Hittite counterpart, Hattusilis III, signed what historians have termed the world's first non-aggression pact between two super-powers. A copy of that document adorns the lobby of the United Nations building in New York City. It includes not only extradition clauses, but also mutual defense provisions should either side be threatened by a third party. Archaeological confirmation of these mutually beneficial relationships has recently been excavated by members of the expedition sponsored by the Roemer-Pelizaeus Museum of Hildesheim, Germany, at Kantir. Here, in this Egyptian city in the eastern Delta which served as a Rameside residence, they found evidence for the ancient manufacture of specifically Hittite weapons which were crafted together with typically Egyptian chariots, suggesting that Hittite soldiers of rank were peacefully resident in the court of Rameses II.

Rameses II was one of the longest lived pharaohs ever to have ruled Egypt. He ruled for over sixty years, and therefore had plenty of time to engage in myriad building programs throughout the land. His reinscribing of many of the monuments of his predecessors, termed usurpation, may be regarded as a symbolic attempt on his part to integrate himself into the monuments of those predecessors.

There is yet another dimension to this building mania. The sheer, superhuman scale of many of his own monuments (pages 116-117) may be understood as a very poignant answer to the question, "where has the glory of Egypt gone?" Rameses II and others of his age doubtless realized that the events at the end of Dynasty 18, precipitated by the Amarna pharaohs, and the threatened world order brought about in Dynasty 19 by the Hittite presence in the Syria-Palestine

Merenptah, son of Rameses II, erected a stela to commemorate a successful campaign against the Sea Peoples; the stela contains the first known mention of Israel: "Libya is destroyed, the Hittite empire is at peace, Canaan is devastated... Israel is laid waste, its seed exists no more..."

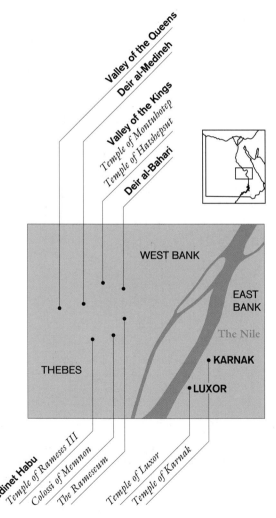

region, fundamentally altered the ancient Egyptian worldview. The glory days of Dynasty 4, with its massive pyramids and gigantic Sphinx, and the undisputed position of world authority enjoyed by the Egyptians under Tuthmoses III and Amunhotep III, for example, had somehow slipped away. Rameses II, in an attempt to reclaim some of that lost ground, asserted himself in the one way readily available to him – the commissioning of architectural programs rivaling, in sheer scale, those of the pharaohs of Dynasty 4.

Sety I had arranged for Rameses II, while still crown prince, to marry Nefertari, who was several years older than the prince. It has been cogently argued that Nefertari was herself a descendant of the powerful Theban elite. This marriage was an attempt on the part of Sety I to bring the Theban elite back into the fold of his Rameside family, whose principal residence was now in the eastern Delta, far removed from the river valley at Thebes. The marriage was a fruitful partnership because Nefertari played a very prominent role in the affairs of state. She is known to have both written to, and exchanged gifts with, Queen Pudukhepa, the wife of the Hittite king, Hattusilis III. Her tomb in the Valley of the Queens is remarkable for the quality of some of its painted decoration, which is without precedent in Egyptian art. Moreover, the religious program of the temples at Abu Simbel, revealed by the inscriptions, demonstrates that Nefertari continued to perform the functions associated with the Divine Wife of Amun, as inaugurated by Ahmosesnefertari at the beginning of Dynasty 18. The similarity of the names, together with other autobiographical data, strongly suggests that Nefertari was related to that queen and may very well have been in addition a half-sister of Nefertiti (pages 104-105), the wife of Akhenaton.

So long-lived was Rameses II that many courtiers who served him early in his reign died, and over ten of his sons pre-deceased him as well. He was eventually succeeded by Merenptah, his thirteenth son. Merenptah continued to enjoy cordial relations with the Hittites as a result of the treaty which was still in effect, but had to contend with minor disturbances precipitated by the Kushites to the south and by the Libyans to the east. The Libyan assault upon Egypt was compounded by the presence of those whom the ancient Egyptians called Peoples of the Sea. They were a motley crew of refugees from lands in and around the eastern Mediterranean who had been put to flight by forces too complicated to detail at this time. As they moved from one region to the next they forced others to join their number in a domino effect until the hordes reached the borders of Egypt. It may very well have been the perceived presence of these roving bands which motivated the Hittites and Egyptians to agree to come to each other's defense if threatened by a third party. Hittite aid was not forthcoming, because they, like the Egyptians, were being assaulted by the same kinds of displaced peoples.

Merenptah was successful in repelling the waves of Sea Peoples which attacked the borders of his realm, and erected a stela in his mortuary temple in Thebes to commemorate the event. The stela is important for a number of reasons, not the least of which is the mention for the first time in Egyptian records of the word "Israel." The implication is that Merenptah, because he had successfully defeated the Sea Peoples, brought peace to the region. The text, therefore, suggests that the peoples of the Syria-Palestine area no longer posed a military threat to Egypt. As a result of this monument, Merenptah cannot be considered, as he often is, the pharaoh of the Exodus.

The end of Dynasty 19 is characterized by a series of ephemeral rulers, each vying for control of the land. Many of these individuals aligned themselves to members of the powerful Theban elite who for centuries now had remained loyal to the cult of Amun, and looked forward to the day when they would again be able to assert themselves as rulers of the land. The transition from Dynasty 19 to 20 appears to have been peacefully effected, although many local Theban officials remained in office. Rameses III, the second and most important pharaoh of the dynasty, was confronted once again by the onslaught of Sea Peoples. Time and again Rameses III battled these individuals, each time gaining victories, but each time finding his realm flooded by untold numbers of displaced peoples, foremost among whom were the Libyans. Their presence in Egypt was too great to ignore, and many of these Libyans were settled in communities throughout Egypt where they would finally organize themselves into independent polities and rival the Egyptians themselves for control of Egypt.

Rameses III also found himself threatened from within. His harem included several women of foreign origin, some presumed to have been Syrian. Soon a plot was hatched by a secondary wife who sought to assassinate Rameses III in an effort to secure the throne of Egypt for her son. The plot was planned on a grand scale, and listed among the conspirators not only other women of the harem, but also major administrators of the realm and a general of the army. All means were at the disposal of the conspirators, including magic, and, from the surviving records of the trials against the conspirators which were held during the reign of Rameses IV, they appear to have been successful. These texts have all the makings of a modern courtroom drama. Five of the judges of the court were themselves accused of favoring some of the female defendants, with whom they were allegedly having sex. In the end, no less than 17 of the conspirators were executed; one was ordered to commit suicide; and still others had their noses and ears cut off. One received a reprimand and was released.

The affair was an unsettling one, and demonstrated to all the vulnerability of the monarch and the power which could be amassed by disaffected members of the elite. Throughout Egypt, but more particularly at Thebes, local administrators successfully set themselves up as petty monarchs, often as rivals of pharaoh himself. At the same time, members of certain Libyan enclaves, taking advantage of an unsettled political situation, did the same.

The central authority of the land had begun to unravel. Toward the end of the dynasty, the Egyptians even witnessed the blatant entry and plundering of many of the royal tombs in the Valley of the Kings. Although these sacrilegious thefts are attributed to bands of marauding Libyans, their numbers included high ranking Egyptian officials at Thebes. The guilty were brought to trial, as recorded in the preserved Tomb Robberies Papyrus. Despite the fact that seventeen thieves were found guilty and were executed by impaling on a stake, future robbers were not deterred. Once again, tombs in both the Valley of the Kings and in the Valley of the Queens were entered and looted of their goods.

The chaos and anarchy which followed plunged Egypt into the next stage in its remarkable history, the Third Intermediate Period.

Toward the end of Dynasty 19 and throughout Dynasty 20 Egypt was beset by troubles; the Sea Peoples continued to attack; Libyans flooded into Egypt; and Rameses III was apparently assassinated by members of his court. The country descended into anarchy, which signalled the end of the New Kingdom.

**The Colossal Statue, reinscribed
for Rameses II, at Memphis
Red granite; 297" in height**
The epic tale of the decision to raise
the funds necessary for the restoration
of this colossal statue, and the
sequence of negotiations which
resulted in its packing and shipping
to the United States so that it could
be unveiled to an eager American
audience as part of the inaugural
festivities of the special exhibition
Rameses the Great, which opened
on April 15, 1987 in the City
of Memphis, Tennessee, has been
recounted elsewhere.
Today, that this statue stands erect
and proud, its height dominating the
eastern end of the open air museum
at Mitrahineh, ancient Memphis, is
due in no small part to those efforts.
The sheer size of the image, dwarfing
many of the trees which line the
garden in which it stands, is indicative
of one of the most salient
characteristics of ancient Egyptian art
and architecture–mass and
superhuman scale rolled into one.
Although that characteristic is
associated singly with the reign of
Rameses II and collectively with the
pharaohs of the Old Kingdom, whose
Great Pyramids and Sphinx on
the Giza Plateau are without rival
anywhere in the world, other
pharaohs and other dynasties created
monuments which equally combine
mass and superhuman scale. The
pharaohs of the Middle Kingdom
were among them, as the still extant
masonry bases which supported a pair
of colossal statues erected at Bihmu in
the Faiyum for Pharaoh Amunemhat
III suggest. These are estimated
to have been about 480" in height,
about 40% taller than this colossus
of Rameses II, and the lower portion
of one of them was still to be seen in
1672 by some of the first, and most
intrepid, European visitors to the
land of the Nile.
It has been cogently suggested,
in fact, that the Memphis colossus
of Rameses II was originally designed
and sculpted for one of these kings
of the Middle Kingdom, and that
it was subsequently appropriated by
Rameses II, who ordered his
craftsmen to reinscribe the statue
with his inscriptions.
The statue looms ever taller the closer
one gets to it. Approaching this
colossus today, the sense of one's own
smallness in comparison becomes
overwhelming. That shrinking feeling
is reinforced by the clever way in
which the ancient Egyptian craftsmen
fashioned the eyes. They are sculpted
so that they sit slanted in their sockets,
conveying the very real impression
that pharaoh, proud and supreme,
is looking down on his subjects.

**Statuette of Pharaoh Rameses II
offering a triad** (overleaf)
**New Kingdom, Dynasty 19
Graywacke; 15 3/8" in length
From Thebes; CG 42144**
This statuette represents a prostrate
Rameses II proffering a triad set upon
a shrine. Its inscriptions have been
cut with a jeweler's precision, and
their lighter color, a direct result
of that cutting, was intentional and
meant to contrast with the matt
polish which was applied to the rest
of the greenish stone. The statuette,
despite its seductive appeal, can really
be seen as a subtle ideological
statement. It has already been
established that members of the elite
enjoyed using visual puns in order
to circumvent conventions (page 70).
Pharaohs, likewise, were guilty of such
circumventions, and often
commissioned works such as this,
the veiled message of which would,
of course, be understood by the
other learned members of the elite.
That message is in the form of
a rebus, or visual pun.
The group of deities which Rameses
II proffers are to be identified
as a hawk-headed deity, whose value
as a hieroglyph is read "re".

A second figure is identified as the
god Amun, intended to be read as
"amun". The third figure is a child
god, whose hieroglyphic value is read
"moses". All three are resting on
a hieroglyph representing an irrigation
canal, which is read "mery". These
four images, while ostensibly forming
part of a triad intended to receive the
veneration of pharaoh, are actually
one of the names of the king himself,
pronounced something on the order
of "Ramesesmeryamun".
This statuette is, therefore, a religious
statement in which Rameses II,
because he is worshipping himself in
the form of his own name, reaffirms
his own divinity. It is a visual
proclamation to all that Rameses II
is a god. By understanding how such
a rebus works, the connection
between ancient Egyptian art and
hieroglyphs becomes easier to
comprehend.

**Head of the God Amun
New Kingdom, Dynasty 19
Rose granite; 38 1/2" in height
From Tanis; 26/5/8/11**
During Dynasties 19 and 20, the
Rameside pharaohs maintained several
residences in the eastern Delta.
As time passed, the branch of the Nile
River along which some of these
settlements were established began
to silt up. As a result, these earlier
settlements were gradually abandoned
in favor of the site of Tanis, which
became an important strategic and
commercial center because of its
location on Lake Manzala. The city
rose to prominence during the course
of Dynasties 21 and 22 (pages 178-
187). The pharaohs of these two
dynasties, seeking to embellish the
new city with statues, obelisks, and
temples as rapidly as possible, reverted
to the ancient Egyptian custom
of usurping, or appropriating, earlier
monuments. Many of the statues
at Tanis, therefore, were transported
to this city from sites abandoned
at the end of the Rameside Period
because of the silting up of that
branch of the Nile.
This head, now broken from its
body, belonged to a statue moved
to Tanis from an earlier Delta site.
The god represented can be identified
as Amun, by virtue of the two tall
plumes which serve as his headdress.
By means of such usurpations, the
ancient Egyptians were constantly
reminded of their past. This interest
in their own history is evident as well
in the funerary furnishings of the
royal tombs at Tanis. Pharaoh
Psusennes I (page 183) was buried
with an ewer inscribed for Ahmoses,
who was remembered for liberating
Egypt from the Hyksos yoke.

43698

Relief of Pharaoh Rameses II
New Kingdom, Dynasty 19
Sandstone; 23 5/8" in height
From Thebes; JE 43698
The mass and super-human scale
of ancient Egyptian sculpture is more
accessible to the exhibition visitor,
for the obvious reason that statues are
more easily moved (page 122) than
entire temples. It is for this reason
that examples of temple reliefs, such
as this panel which was originally part
of the walls of the Rameseum, or
mortuary temple of Rameses II (pages
116-117), are here included.
The pharaoh is shown wearing what
is often called the Blue Crown, once
identified as a kind of battle helmet.
During the course of the New
Kingdom this accessory had lost most
of its bellicose associations and was
worn by pharaoh in those ceremonies
which required his active, physical
participation. The crown is
characterized by the repeated loops
of the body of the uraeus.
The facial features of the king are
indebted to those developed for
certain images of Amunhotep III
(page 100). These include the
almond-shaped eyes and the so-called
rings of Venus, in the form of three
flesh folds on his neck. One recalls
that in the Kings' List at Abydos,
commissioned by his father Sety I, the
names of Hatshepsut and the Amarna
Pharaohs had been excised, but that
of Amunhotep III was retained. That
retention is manifest in this relief,
visually linking Rameses II to one
of the accepted pharaohs of Egypt's
history, who occurs in the Kings' List
as an immediate predecessor of the
Rameside pharaohs of Dynasty 19.

Block statue of the Treasury
Official Benemeret and the
Princess Meretamun
New Kingdom, Dynasty 19
Gray granite; 27 1/2" in height
From Thebes; CG 42171
Almost no other pre-Greek
civilization of the ancient Near East
expressed in its art a love for its
children in exactly the same way
as did ancient Egyptian art. Examples
from the Middle Kingdom (page 70)
and Dynasty 18 (pages 104-106)
paved the way for depictions such
as this. The official Benemeret held
high posts in the administration,
but particularly in the treasury of the
realm: *the hereditary prince and*
count... the overseer of the twin houses
of gold, overseer of the twin houses of
silver... In addition, he was pharaoh's
confidant and trusted friend: *...the*
one who fills the heart of the king in the
king's splendid monuments, the one who
is ever in the heart of the good god...
Doubtless because of those qualities,
pharaoh, suggested to have been none
other than Rameses II, entrusted
the daughter of the king, beloved of her
father, Meretamun to the loving care
of this conscientious official.
The block statue, so called because
its contours closely conform to
the perimeter of the block of stone
from which it was sculpted, was
an appropriate choice for this
representation. Its cubic shape
envelops Meretamun within the
protective embrace of Benemeret.
Her head, identified as that of a child
by means of the side lock (page 70),
which breaks the composition's
symmetry, was skillfully designed
so that it would not obscure the face
of her guardian behind it.

ANCIENT EGYPTIAN PAINTING

Just as the ancient Egyptians gave names to the Great Pyramids of the Old and Middle Kingdoms, so did they name virtually every other building they ever constructed. And so it happened that here in Western Thebes, in a district modernly called Medinet Habu, they erected a temple in which the funerary cult of the deceased pharaoh Rameses III could be celebrated, and named it *The Mansion of Millions of Years of Pharaoh Rameses III, United with Eternity in the Estate of the God Amun.* Egyptologists are unanimous in their assessment that, after those at Edfu and Dendera, this is the best preserved temple in Egypt. This temple formed part of a larger complex, which was entered through a fortified gateway set into the eastern enclosure wall, the tops of which featured crenelations. Although of rounded form, these crenelations strikingly recall those found along the tops of medieval castles and keeps in Europe. These features may be regarded as an indication of the period's troubled times, because Rameses III was constantly engaged in battles against the Sea Peoples. The gateway gives way to a large court, leading to a second of somewhat smaller dimensions, behind which is a complex warren of cult rooms. Traveling the route along the temple's main axis pharaoh and the high priests would make their way into and out of the holy of holies. The floral-form columns provide the illusion of the primeval swamp, so eloquently recreated by the Hypostyle Hall at Karnak (pages 86-87). In keeping with the basic plan of most Egyptian temples, the sequence of courts and rooms along the central axis are characterized by a perceptible progression of ever decreasing areas of space. This is achieved by raising the floor level, with a concomitant lowering of the ceiling level, the intent of which was to recreate a sense of the primeval mound which rose from the waters on the first day of creation (pages 198-199). Remains of the royal palace, which are rarely so well preserved, occupy the southern side of the complex. Its rooms are directly connected to the temple by means of a series of doorways. It was doubtless here in life that Rameses III interacted with those members of his harem who ultimately conspired to assassinate him.

Although it is difficult to convey to the visitor to such an exhibition of ancient Egyptian art an adequate sense of architecture, it is somewhat easier to present an overview of ancient Egyptian painting, since spectacularly painted works of art can be exhibited in galleries. The following discussion is intended only as an overview of this complex topic, concentrating on a few characteristics of New Kingdom painting.

The ancient Egyptians had very early on developed a system of representing each object from its most characteristic point of view. That depiction was dependent upon a contour line, which, for the sake of comparison, is here compared to the black lines with which the images in a child's coloring book are often reproduced. This comparison is intended neither to be disparaging nor to suggest in any way that ancient Egyptian painting is childlike. It is offered to make a point. Namely, that ancient Egyptian color was generally applied in such a way that colors almost never bleed over these contour lines from one form to another. The painted wooden coffin panel of Middle Kingdom date (pages 132-133) is a representative example of this phenomenon. The colors employed for the hieroglyphs in the line of inscriptions across the top, as well as for the funerary items in the so-called frieze, or horizontal register, of objects have been contained within their respective contour lines. Such an approach to color characterizes not only painting and relief, but also sculpture and architecture.

During the course of the New Kingdom, these conventions were still employed for the decoration of the painted tombs at Thebes, which are admirably represented here by the funerary vignettes in the tomb of Ramose (pages 134-135, 138, and 140-141), who served as both a governor and vizier under pharaoh Akhenaton. Certain details within these vignettes, however, reveal that the consortium of elite designers, headed by pharaoh himself, were developing a repertoire of techniques which were to contribute to the creation, during Dynasties 19 and 20, of some of the most remarkable paintings ever created in ancient Egypt.

One of those techniques was that developed for depicting crowds, as can be seen in the detail from the tomb of Ramose (pages 134-135). Because of the requirement that each element in any given scene had to retain its visual integrity and could not be obscured, crowd scenes might be represented as groups of people on two different levels or, as here, as over-lapping figures of alternating hues of the same color, splayed out as one might fan open playing cards. The alternation of color contributes to the unmistakable visual clarity of each figure represented in such a group.

A second feature was also developed, the intention of which was to indicate as clearly as possible the effects of a gossamer fabric passing over the body. In another vignette from the Tomb of Ramose (page 138) one sees how the effect of the finely woven linen garments passing over the body has been achieved. Where the flesh of the legs and arms is not covered, the hue is a darker red. In those passages in which the costume covers the body, the flesh of the figures is rendered as a lighter pink color. The paint, in both of these techniques, is still applied in conformity to the requirements of the contour line.

These, then, were the techniques used in the decoration of the paintings in the tombs of both the members of the elite at Thebes and in the Valley of the Kings. A stela from the city of Amarna (pages 136-137) is painted within that same tradition and exhibits many of the same features, including the use of a yellow background, which are characteristic of the painted scenes in the Tomb of Tutankhamun. Despite the fact that one cannot visit that tomb at a moment's notice, this wonderful stela is a surprisingly accurate reflection of the figures in the decoration of that tomb, and for present purposes may be profitably regarded as its miniature version. This is not simply a boast, because it is known that that pharaoh, as Tutankhaton, grew up at Amarna before moving to Thebes, restoring the position of Amun, and changing his name to Tutankhamun.

A further technical development is seen in the painted treatment of the bodies of the figures in a second stela of late New Kingdom date (page 139). Here the requirement that color should stay rigidly fixed within its contour line has been relaxed, so that the honey-colored browns of the flesh tones, more prominently visible in the bodies of the three kneeling figures in the bottom register, are applied in such a way that they bleed, or run. This development may be regarded as a furthering of the tradition of depicting the body beneath the garment as a lighter hue.

The ultimate utilization of this technical development can be found on a figural ostrakon, or painted limestone flake, found in the Tomb of Rameses VI in the Valley of the Kings. The art historical interest in this image resides in the treatment of the skin tones of the face, which are represented as a series of shading, as if the king were wearing rouge. That shading is a direct violation of the laws of the contour line and reveals that the ancient Egyptian craftsmen-painters were capable of achieving an extraordinarily life-like effect in a limited number of circumstances. However, the best examples of this technique on a large scale are to be found in a selected few images in the tomb of Nefertari, wife of Rameses II, in the Valley of the Queens (access to which is strictly limited).

It should be remembered, therefore, that the greatest achievements in ancient Egyptian art occurred not during the Amarna Period, but during the Rameside Period of Dynasties 19 and 20.

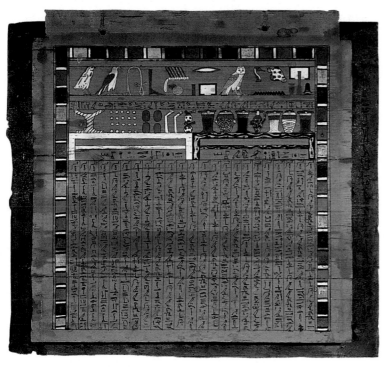

**Side panel from a coffin inscribed
for Buau and Montuhotep**
Middle Kingdom, Dynasty 12
Painted wood; 25 1/2" in height
From Thebes; CG 28027

In addition to revealing the artistic
tenets by which color was generally
applied so as not to violate the
contours, or outlines, of the
individual hieroglyphs and objects,
the use of color also shows how the
ancient Egyptian craftsmen-painters
could imitate in pigment a wide
variety of materials. The depiction
of the stones from which the vessels
on the right of the panel were
hollowed out and the representation
of the wooden piece of furniture to
the left reveal that these individuals
could imitate in paint almost any
material found in nature.

This coffin is fascinating for a number
of reasons. The first is that it is
inscribed for two different individuals.
The inscriptions on the front, or
outside, name the owner as Buau,
whereas those on the inside name him
as Montuhotep. Although it is, one
supposes, theoretically possible that
both could have been buried in this
coffin, a better explanation seems to
be that the coffin was commissioned
for one Buau, but was never
delivered. It remained there until
there was a need for a coffin for
Montuhotep. Whereupon the coffin

was purchased, the way one would
buy a garment off-the-rack, and
altered by adding inscriptions and the
name of Montuhotep on the inside.
A careful examination of the right
edge of this panel (detail, left), which
has been mitered to fit more snugly
into the long side panel, reveals the
traces of a funerary inscription.
This is visible now that the coffin is
dismantled, but would of course have
been hidden from sight when the
coffin was used to contain the
mummy. Almost no one would have
been able to guess that there was
an inscription in this place and no one
would have been able to see or read
it. The text is funerary in nature, and
is there magically to insure the
protection of the deceased. In the
event the painting on the interior and
exterior were effaced or damaged, the
deities would magically know that
this spell was here, where its message
could be eternally invoked for the
benefit of the deceased.

**Scene from the Tomb of Ramose,
Governor and Vizier under
Pharaoh Akhenaton** (overleaf)
Western Thebes

Many of the techniques of painting
developed during the course of
Dynasty 18 are evident in this scene,
painted on one of the limestone
walls of the tomb of Ramose. In this
vignette there is an interest in the
wailing women, mourners at the
funeral of Ramose, who express the
grief of family members and close
friends by their gestures. The
craftsmen-painters have indicated the
tears of bereavement cascading down
the cheeks of some of the participants
as a series of three dotted lines. These
are clearly made out on the faces of
several of the woman at the left-hand
side of the composition.

The suggestion of a crowd scene
is achieved by a convention described
as "above is behind." The figures
at the back are not to be understood
as being taller than those in the front
row, but are better understood as if
standing on risers, like members of
a choral group during a performance.
In this way the visual integrity of
each figure is maintained while the
appearance of a crowd scene
is suggested.

Magical stela of the Goddess Isis and the God Shed (left; this page, 3 details from sides of stela)
New Kingdom, Dynasty 18
Painted limestone; 17 5/8" in height
From Amarna; JE 46954

Although some popular accounts still maintain that the religion, devoted to the aton, as introduced under Amunhotep III and practised at Amarna during the reign of his son and successor, Akhenaton, was monotheistic, a strict, religious definition of that term reveals the contrary. Other deities were worshipped there as well, to judge from the number of amulets and different objects, such as this stela, which were excavated at the city of Amarna. These objects indicate that the inhabitants of Amarna were interested in maintaining those deities and ancient traditions which offered them a modicum of protection against evils of every kind. The subject matter and prayers on this stela belong to that tradition as well. To the left stands the god Shed, who grasps a scorpion and two arrows in his hands. He is wearing the side lock of youth. An offering table separates him from Isis, depicted at the right, who holds a mace and a bow, and carries a basket suspended from her arm. The presence of the scorpion may be interpreted on several levels. On one level it is a venomous beast whose sting is potentially lethal. On a second level, the scorpion was associated with magic (page 76). Its appearance here in the hands

of a youth who is also holding a pair of arrows is clear. Invocations and prayers to Shed will magically protect the petitioner in the same way that Shed, armed with his arrows, is protected from the sting of the scorpion he holds. That message is reinforced both by the presence of the goddess Isis, who herself is armed, and by the spells represented by the hieroglyphs.

This stela is important because its narrow sides are decorated with miniature scenes in relief (above). On the right, narrow side of the stela, in the upper register, one standing, female figure can be seen offering a lotus to a second, seated one. Below is depicted a dancing girl and seated harper. The left side, decorated with only one register, represents a seated woman again being presented with an offering by a second female figure. All of these scenes relate to contemporary offering scenes found in the tombs of members of the elite at Thebes. One can, therefore, suggest that the magical protection afforded in this context by Shed and Isis has funereal associations. For those who cannot readily travel to Egypt in order to visit the Tomb of Tutankhamun, the entrance to which is regulated by the imposition of a surcharge, this stela is the next best thing. The gold color of the background and the depiction of the god Shed are identical, in many respects, to the depictions of Tutankhamun in that tomb. These include the seemingly

discordant proportion of the head relative to the body and pot belly. Shed is so depicted because the conventions of ancient Egyptian art specify that depictions of deities should conform to those of pharaohs (page 100). And it is known that Tutankhamun was resident at Amarna, where he lived under the name of Tutankhaton, until he moved to Thebes, changed his name, and restored the worship of Amun.

Magical stela of the God Shed dedicated by Peherepezet
New Kingdom, Dynasty 20
Painted limestone; 11 1/2" in height
From Thebes; JE 43569

This stela was discovered, together with several others, in the southwestern part of Western Thebes, modernly called Deir al Medineh. Here was located a village, the principal inhabitants of which were the craftsmen who were co-opted by the elite to work on the royal tombs in the Valley of the Kings. This stela was dedicated by one of those craftsmen, Peherepezet, whose only title is "Servant," which is the equivalent, in this particular context, of craftsman. Peherepezet does not specify his craft specialization and, in keeping with the anonymity of features of Egyptian society as a whole, passes over in silence the name of the pharaoh under whom he worked.

The stela, remarkable for the painterly treatment of the body which violates the requirements of the contour line, depicts a train of four deities, enthroned, at the top. These are identified as Ptah, Sobek, Isis, and Meretseger. Ptah, although originally from Memphis, became the patron of craftsmen. Meretseger, whose name means "she-who-loves-silence," was one of the goddesses associated with the Theban cemeteries, in which the silence of the dead reigned supreme. She is shown with her characteristic head in the form of a serpent.

The lower register, observing primacy of place at the spectator's left, affords that honor to Shed (page 136), who here grasps a lance and serpents in his left hand and a scorpion in his right. He is invoked for his magical powers of protection, which the entire family expected to enjoy, even the daughter who is shown to the far right, with an elaborate coiffure reminiscent of the two ponytails worn by Nebhethenetesen (page 78).

Scene from the Tomb of Ramose, Governor and Vizier under Pharaoh Akhenaton (pages 140-141)
Western Thebes

The vignette illustrated here shows how another technique developed for the depiction of crowd scenes was employed. The offering bearers associated with the funeral procession of Ramose are identical with respect to their contour, or outline. They have been arranged along a register, or groundline, and are fanned out, the way one might separate playing cards held in a bridge game.

In order for each figure to be clearly visible, the craftsmen-painters have employed alternating hues of the same color to depict the flesh tones of adjacent figures.

Scene from the Tomb of Ramose, Governor and Vizier under Pharaoh Akhenaton
Western Thebes

This vignette from the Tomb of Ramose demonstrates how the craftsmen-painters achieved the effect of permitting the body to show through garments. In certain instances, as here, the fine linen, from which such sheer fabrics were woven, was responsible for a change of hue. The male skin, not covered by this linen, is a deeper red, which changes to a rosy-pink when covered by garments woven of that material. It is remarkable to observe that the finest of such fine linen garments have been found to contain 160 threads per inch, in contrast to the finest modern woven textiles which average only about 120 threads to the inch. The existence of such sheer weaves doubtless contributed to their depiction in art. Moreover, these gossamer fabrics enabled the craftsmen-painters to explore the revelation of the body beneath the drapery in a way which anticipates the Greek achievement almost one thousand years later, as exemplified in the statues of the goddesses from the pediments of the Parthenon, now in the British Museum in London.

THE THIRD INTERMEDIATE PERIOD

Previous page
**View of the Chapel
of Osiris-Wenenefer
Third Intermediate Period
Dynasty 25
Karnak**
Although the Third Intermediate Period witnessed the fragmentation of Egypt's central authority and its division into two politically competing geographic spheres of influence, the arrival of the Kushites from Africa did restore a semblance of order, particularly at Thebes. Arriving as warriors, fully convinced of their role as avengers against those who continued to blaspheme against the gods, the Kushites in Egypt championed the worship of Amun, whose cult was the source of particular pride in their country, Kush, or Nubia, centered around the Fourth Cataract.

At Thebes the Kushites aligned themselves so closely with the elite members of the Theban priesthood that their daughters served as Divine Wives of the god Amun. That association was effected in the following way.

When the Kushite pharaoh Piankhy arrived in Thebes, the reigning Egyptian monarch was king Osorkon III, whose own daughter, Shepenwepet I, was serving as the Divine Wife of the god Amun. Piankhy compelled Osorkon III into accepting an arrangement whereby Shepenwepet I would adopt his own Kushite daughter, Amunirdis, known as the elder, and enroll her into the office. Shepenwepet I then exercised her authority until her natural death, at which time Amunirdis the Elder assumed the position.

This chapel was erected by Shepenwepet I and the Kushite Amunirdis the Elder (pages 156-157). Its reliefs commemorate the peaceful cooperation between the Divine Wife of Amun and her adopted Kushite daughter. By means of these smooth transitions, commemorated in such monuments, power passed between the Kushites and the members of the Egyptian elite. Some semblance of order was finally restored to Egypt, at least as far as Memphis in the North. Amunirdis the Elder then enrolled her natural daughter in the same office (pages 150-151) so that the Kushite line might continue unbroken.

The Third Intermediate Period was brought about by the dissolution of central authority and the concomitant rise of powerful members of local elites, as well as by the assertive presence of the Libyans whose numbers in Egypt increased during the course of Dynasties 19 and 20. The picture of Egypt at this time is one of cultural decay, political impotence, and international incompetence. The Old Testament aptly sums up Egypt's international role in these terms: *Behold, you are putting your trust in the staff of this broken reed, on Egypt, upon which if anyone should lean, it will go into the hand and pierce it.*

Egyptian documents, contemporary with the period, do not differ markedly in their sentiments about the depths to which the esteem and prestige of Egypt had plunged. One such document, while admittedly a romance penned at the end of the Rameside Period, is nonetheless instructive in this regard. It deals with the misadventures of an Egyptian official named Wenamun, who is dispatched by the priests of the god Amun on a trading expedition to obtain cedar from Lebanon for the cult of Amun at Thebes. The tale begins with Wenamun's journey from Thebes to the Delta. (The reader soon learns that Egypt is now divided into two realms: Upper Egypt, controlled by the priests of the god Amun, and the Delta, ruled over by Libyan princes. The members of the hereditary elite in Upper Egypt, who can be traced back to Dynasty 18, and who were involved in the struggles between the supporters of Amun and those of the Aton, were finally vindicated. Their successors emerged during the course of the Third Intermediate Period as rulers of Egypt, although admittedly not of the entire country.)

Wenamun is forced to travel through the land of the Delta princes, whose capital city was at Tanis (pages 178-187). When he finally reaches his destination on the Asiatic coast of the cedar forests, Wenamun is shabbily treated, despite his attempts to gain respect by reminding everyone of the lucrative nature of Egyptian mercantile activity in the past. After enduring several humiliations, Wenamun sets sail with his cargo, but is driven by the wind to a remote island, perhaps to be identified with Cyprus. There, sitting despondently on the shore, Wenamun watches the southern flight toward Egypt of the migratory birds, and wishing he were one of them, wonders whether he will ever see his beloved Thebes again.

The account is instructive. Egypt's position in the international community had indeed fallen, and her political clout in the Syria-Palestine region had assuredly waned. Nevertheless, to paint such a picture of Egypt during the Third Intermediate Period, relying exclusively on such sources, fails to do justice to the significant, but often overlooked, achievements of the Egyptians of the period.

To begin with, although the political authority of the country was divided between the courts of the Delta princes and the high priests of Amun at Thebes, the material culture of the nation as a whole appears to have been very homogeneous. That observation has troubled commentators inasmuch as the petty princes of the Delta were Libyans, and the Third Intermediate Period ended with Dynasty 25, the kings of which were assuredly Blacks, who had assumed the reigns of government from the priest-kings of Amun by means of military conquest. Were it not for names and titles, as well as for a few outward trappings, the ethnicity of both the Libyans and the Nubians, or Kushites as the Black kings are known (pages 148-151), could not be gleaned from the archaeological record. In other words, in ancient Egypt the ethnicity of any particular foreign cultural group is always subsumed beneath a thick veneer of Egyptian culture. The reason for this may be profitably ascribed to the resilience of the Egyptian elite, whose members, in order to preserve their advantaged status in life, entered into complicity with their foreign overlords by revealing to them the advantages of maintaining the status quo relative to the members of the elite. These foreigners were then co-opted into the system and shared, on an equal footing with the original members of the elite, in that advantaged position. Once co-opted the foreigners would shed their own ethnicity and don all of the cultural expressions of the members of the Egyptian elite, becoming, in the process, more Egyptian than the Egyptians themselves. It is for this reason that it is so difficult to identify, within the archaeological record, elements in the culture of the Third Intermediate Period which are decidedly either Libyan or Kushite. This shedding of foreign ethnicity contributed to the uniformity of ancient Egypt's material culture during the course of the Third Intermediate Period.

With the Libyans, and to a far greater extent the Kushites, behaving as if they were more Egyptian than the members of the Egyptian elite, Egyptian culture of the Third Intermediate Period developed in some remarkable ways, each of which may be regarded as the culmination of pre-existing Egyptian technologies.

Foremost among these technologies was the craft of mummification, which reached its zenith during the course of the early Third Intermediate Period. The high quality of the mummification process may be regarded in terms of the pious actions of the high priests of Amun at Thebes during this period. In the aftermath of the tomb robberies, which occurred at the close of the Rameside Period, the priest-kings of Thebes took it upon themselves to collect and reinter the vandalized corpses of their illustrious forefathers. Pinodjem II, who ruled at Thebes at the same time as the Libyan kings of Dynasty 21 at Tanis, reinterred about forty of his ancestors, including Rameses II, in an earlier tomb which he ordered to be enlarged for this purpose. He seems to have been following the lead of Pinodjem I who had earlier reinterred other mummified pharaohs in the tomb of Amunhotep II (pages 172-173) in the Valley of the Kings. It has even been seriously suggested that tombs not plundered by robbers were intentionally entered by official decree during this period, with a two-fold purpose in mind. The first was to demonstrate the futility of continued robbing, since the tombs would have been already emptied of their contents, and the mummies reverentially reinterred elsewhere in secret caches. The second was so that the valuables recovered might be recycled into the official economy of the state.

All the breaking into and entering of tombs which occurred during this period should be sufficient evidence to indicate that the ancient Egyptians themselves were little concerned about the curses allegedly cast over such burials, intended to punish those who violated the sepulchers of the dead. Clearly, putative curses of the variety which the symbolists attribute as being the cause of the untimely death of Lord Carnarvon, following his penetration of the tomb of Tutankhamun, would have been more efficacious, had they existed, among the ancient Egyptians themselves. The ancient texts dealing with the circumstances of these tomb robberies pass over in silence all mention of such curses. The perpetrators do not die suddenly as a result of their entering the tombs; they die because they are sentenced to death by the courts. This is not to say that curses directed against those who would profane a tomb or destroy a statue did not exist in ancient Egypt:

As to all persons, all scribes, all commoners... who will remove the statue... and

In the Third Intermediate Period political authority in Egypt was divided between the Libyan princes of the Delta and the Theban elite.

obliterate its writing, they shall fall prey to the wrath of Amun the Great and shall be subject to the ferocity of the king... As for those who do not utter these words [contained in the funerary prayers for the deceased], the Mistress of the West will cause them to be sick and their wives to become afflicted. As to anyone who removes this papyrus... he will receive the abomination of the crocodile god Sobek...

The force of such texts is self-evident in the context of the ancient Egyptian social system, which stressed the importance of a morally upright, ethical life. Such violations were, consequently, regarded as abominations, acts against the accepted social order. The texts were intended, therefore, to tweak the conscience. Most Egyptians respected the tombs of their ancestors; many did not. Of that number, some were caught, tried, and punished with death. For the desired goal of such curses was, in the end, nothing more than a straightforward reprimand: good persons simply do not engage in such activity.

However, the mass interments of this period were not limited to caches of mummies recovered from plundered tombs. Priests of the Theban god Montu, as well as the chief priests of Theban Amun, appeared to have been interred respectively in mass tombs, the former containing 71 sarcophagi, the latter over 150, together with approximately 200 statues.

Certain craft industries flourished during this period as well. Among these was the burgeoning of the so-called faience industry, a glazed, ceramic material similar to porcelain, which seemed to be localized at certain Libyan centers such as Tanis.

More important, however, was the development of highly sophisticated metallurgical technologies which resulted in the meteoric rise of the finely crafted metals which characterize the funerary finds from Tanis (pages 178-187). Whereas almost everyone conversant with ancient Egypt appears to be awed by the discovery of the tomb of Tutankhamun and its treasures, few people realize that the treasure of Tutankhamun is not a unique occurrence within Egyptian archaeology. More lavish in many respects than the objects found in his tomb are those recovered from an entire royal cemetery, found at the site of Tanis, in which some of the kings of Dynasties 21 and 22 were buried. Popular imagination has not been ignited by these spectacular finds because they were made by the Frenchman, Pierre Montet, late in February, 1939. Work continued, but the momentous nature of the find was eclipsed by the outbreak of World War II on September 1, 1939. By the war's end, the world was preoccupied by the Cold War, and Montet's earth-shaking discovery and its paramount importance for the art and civilization of ancient Egypt had passed virtually unnoticed, even by those members of the general public who profess such interest in all things Egyptian. And that is a pity. It is to be hoped, therefore, that the attention devoted to Tanis in *Splendors of Ancient Egypt* will do much to redress this deficiency.

In order to gauge just how important the metallurgical technologies of the ancient Egyptians were during the course of the Third Intermediate Period, consider the following observation. Some of their metalwork was crafted according to the lost wax method, a sophisticated technique whereby the desired form, be it a statue or whatever, was made of wax. The wax was then enveloped in clay which was fired. During that process, the wax melted out, and the clay hardened into terracotta, which was allowed to cool. Thereupon molten metal, usually in the form of bronze, although silver or gold might be used as well, was poured into that cast and took the form of the wax model. The terracotta cast was eventually broken away and the metal object emerged.

The superstitions and legendary curse attached to the opening of the tomb of Tutankhamun in 1922 did not carry such weight with the ancient Egyptians themselves, for whom the inscriptions were no more than admonitions.

Each piece made in this way was one of a kind. More importantly, however, scholars have convincingly demonstrated that this particularly Egyptian way of creating metal objects via the lost wax method was exported to Greece and there, on the island of Samos, incorporated into the technologies of the emerging Greek city-states.

In this light, then, the material culture of Egypt during the Third Intermediate Period assumes a special place in the history of world art, and the negative picture of the period, as outlined at the beginning of this section, must be tempered accordingly.

**Head of a Kushite King,
possibly Shabako
Third Intermediate Period, Dynasty 25
Rose granite; 38 1/4" in height
From Thebes; CG 42010**

The identification of this image as the Kushite pharaoh, Shabako, is provided by the inscription on the back pillar, which contains one of his five names. The king is shown in the traditional guise of an Egyptian pharaoh, wearing the nemes-headdress surmounted by the Double Crown.

A careful examination of the surfaces of this head suggest that it was originally made for a pharaoh of Dynasty 18, which was initially not inscribed. When Shabako became pharaoh, he directed his craftsmen to convert this statue which, it is reasonable to suppose, had already been dedicated in the Karnak temple to his own use by means of two alterations. The first was the cutting of his name on the back pillar. It was not unusual for statues to be dedicated without inscriptions, although it was more common to appropriate statues of earlier monarchs by inscribing them for oneself (page 100).

The second alteration changed the larger, single uraeus on the brow of the original statue into the double uraeus which is now found on Shabako's forehead. The alteration process is distinctly visible, particularly along the vertical cut which separates the hoods of the two serpents. Whereas Egyptologists are still divided about the significance of the double uraeus, as this emblem is called, they are unanimous in their claim that this motif was inextricably associated with the Kushite pharaohs of Dynasty 25. Shabako became pharaoh following the death of his brother, Piankhy. Contemporary sources suggest that he foresaw the dangers of a military confrontation with Assyria, and took initial, but futile, steps to avert such an eventuality.

150

Overleaf (pages 152-153)
**Tomb of Horemheb, Commander
of the armies of Pharaoh
Tutankhamun, erected before he
himself became Pharaoh of Egypt
New Kingdom, Dynasty 18
Sakkara**

The rediscovery of the Memphite
tomb of Horemheb on January 14,
1975, by the joint expedition
of the Egyptian Exploration Society
(London, England) and The
Rijksmuseum van Oudheden (Leiden,
Holland) marked one of those
auspicious occasions in Egyptian
archaeology when a monument,
thought to have been utterly
destroyed by tomb robbers, was
proved to be otherwise.

The initial discovery of the tomb
in the last century is shrouded in
mystery, although blocks, ostensibly
removed at that time, did make their
way into the collections in Leiden.
One learns nothing more about this
tomb until the publication of two
accounts in the 1870s, which seem
to suggest that their authors saw the
tomb, whose location they did not
mention, in the 1850s. Thereafter
its location was concealed beneath
an ever accumulating pile of sand
and debris.

The circumstances which led to the
formation of the joint Anglo-Dutch
mission and the amount of preliminary
study which preceded the actual
commencement of the work have been
recounted elsewhere. Suffice it to say
that fortune smiled on the excavators,
because they had only been in the
field for nine days before they
uncovered a column inscribed with
the names and titles of Horemheb.
That spectacular story of discovery
serves, then, as a backdrop against
which to present an array of minor
arts and an interesting two-
dimensional representation, the
subject matter of which is extremely
interesting (pages 154-159). Whereas
some of these objects have been found
in tombs, or at least can be related
to funerary contexts, there is no good
reason to consider them as objects
of daily use, as more popular accounts
of ancient Egyptian culture continue
to do. The very fact that these objects
were placed in a tomb suggests,
immediately, a religious function.
The objects have been intentionally
selected because they exhibit
variations of a theme, that of the
woman in the marsh. This theme
is so prevalent in Egyptian art and
appears in so many variants in a wide
variety of media over such a
prolonged period, that the theme
must have been a primal one for the
elite members of that society.

**Statue of the Kushite Amunirdis
the Elder, Divine Wife of the
God Amun, made in her honor
by her daughter, Shepenwepet II,
also a Divine Wife of the God Amun
Third Intermediate Period, Dynasty 25
Gray granite; 43 3/4" in height
From Thebes; JE 67871**

The transfer of power at Thebes was
effected when Piankhy, the Kushite
conqueror of Egypt, compelled
Shepenwepet I, daughter of Pharaoh
Osorkon III, who was serving as the
Divine Wife of Amun at Thebes, to
adopt his own daughter, Amunirdis,
and confer upon her the same office
(page 144). When Shepenwepet I
died of natural causes, religious
authority in Thebes passed peacefully
into the hands of the Kushite
pharaohs by virtue of this earlier
adoption. In order to maintain the
preeminent position of the Kushites
among the members of the Theban
elite, Amunirdis the Elder, as this
daughter of Piankhy is known, then
bequeathed the office to her
daughter, Shepenwepet II, perhaps
signifying, by this shared name, that
she was a successor of her foster
grandmother, Shepenwepet I.

It is often claimed that the faces of
the Egyptians, particularly their noses,
were intentionally destroyed by later
generations, in what has been termed
racist acts. The objective of such
intentional disfiguring was, so these
same advocates claim, the removal
of physiognomic features so that the
ethnicity of the ancient Egyptians
could be passed over in silence. Such
positions rarely, if ever, examine the
archaeological context of the statue
in question. In this particular instance
it is known that the statue was reused
in the early Christian Period
as a doorstep, because of the massive
quality of its back pillar. It was
incorporated as such into a house
of the period, face down, in which
position it was discovered in 1937.
The Christian usurpation of this piece
was motivated by a disrespect for the
pagan past, rather than by an attempt
to cover up any ethnic markers.

The close association between these
two Kushite women, mother and
daughter, is eloquently expressed
in the hieroglyphs on the back pillar.
There, one reads, Shepenwepet II
dedicated this statue to her mother
*...so that the name of her mother might
be able to endure forever and ever in
the house of the god Amun...*

Satiric Relief (above; detail, left)
Third Intermediate Period, Dynasty 25
Sandstone; 35 3/4" in length
From Medamoud; JE 58924

This very unusual relief is of fundamental importance for understanding the primal role of the scene of the woman in the swamp, the setting of this vignette. The block originally decorated a temple at Medamoud, not far from Thebes. It is imbued with religious overtones, reinforced by the single column of text to the left: *...[who] is foremost of the kas (spirits) of the living...* The half circles in that text are the hieroglyphs by which the feminine gender is expressed in ancient Egyptian grammar, indicating that "the one who is foremost" is a woman, who may be identified with one of the Kushite Divine Wives of the god Amun (page 151). The Divine Wife is symbolically married to Amun so that her physically human procreative powers might metaphorically unite with those of her male counterpart in order for creation to occur. Creation occurred in a swamp; as a result of creation, harmony was restored and chaos confused.

All of the elements of this creation myth are contained within the swamp scene: a female figure, scantily clad to titillate, playing a harp; a crocodile, rising from the depths of the swamp, in which inherent creation resides, to support the female figure, thereby becoming an integral part of the creative process; the topsy-turvy world of animals in human roles, which may be interpreted as chaos confused and harmony attained as a result of divine creation. So linked in the ancient Egyptian mind were cosmic creation and human birth to resurrection, that all three concepts came to share a common visual vocabulary. Thus the epithet, "foremost of the kas of the living," reaffirms that the generative powers controlled by the Divine Wife of Amun could be readily transferred to funerary practices for the resurrection of the deceased.

Ointment spoon in the form of a female figure in a lotus pond (page 154)
New Kingdom, Dynasty 18
Wood; 9 3/4" in height
From Abu Gurob; CG 45136

The disparate floral forms of this ointment spoon have been harmoniously combined into a pleasing, vertical composition. The lace-like delicacy of the openwork is a tribute to the skill of the wood carver, because ancient Egyptian craftsmen rarely removed the negative material from their work. In this respect the object may be compared to some of the alabaster vessels from the Tomb of Tutankhamun, which share this same characteristic. In keeping with such swamp scenes, the female figure is naked and wears an elaborate wig. The symbolism inherent in the floral forms is reinforced by the use of the color blue, which connotes concepts of rejuvenation and resurrection. The lotus itself is the principal floral motif. As a hieroglyph it puns with the word for "life" (page 70) and was associated with Nun, the personification of the watery abyss from which creation arose. That association is suggested here by the zigzags beneath the female figure's feet, such signs being the hieroglyph for "water." In one version of the creation myth, it was the lotus which rose to the surface, where, when touched by the rays of the sun, its blossom opened for the first time on the first day of creation. This symbolism supports an interpretation that the primary function of objects such as this, in a funerary context, was as a guarantee of resurrection, through analogy with the original creation of the cosmos.

Krateriskos (page 155)
New Kingdom, Dynasty 19
Glass; 3 1/8" in height
From Tanis; JE 49375

Glass was introduced into Egypt around the beginning of the New Kingdom from Mesopotamia where the techniques for its manufacture were first developed. The pharaonic craftsmen immediately recognized the medium's vast potential and soon surpassed their Mesopotamian counterparts in the size, complexity, and colors of their creations. The palm fronds, straw, or animal dung which had been used to fuel the kilns employed in the manufacture of either pottery or faience were incapable of generating the significantly higher temperatures required for the glass industry. That fuel had to be wood, which was very scarce in Egypt. The procurement and distribution of wood appears to have been governed by pharaoh's own administrators who exercised control over many other aspects of the nation's economy as well.

This vessel has been core formed, that is its shape was created beforehand in a different material, around which the glass was then wrapped. When cooled, the core was removed and the interior of the resulting vessel was revealed. Contrary to popular opinion, which credits the Egyptians with its introduction, glass blowing was introduced as a manufacturing technique only during the Roman Imperial Period. The uses to which such vessels were originally put is debatable, but the similarity of some of their forms to vases in other materials suggests that they may have had a like function. In funerary and temple contexts, glass appears to have been valued for its symbolism. The ancient Egyptians believed that the regenerative forces of the sun were manifest in the surfaces of such objects, hence its sheen. These material properties were then compared to the creative potential inherent in the primeval swamp, which, when struck by the sun's rays, resulted in creation.

**Mirror with a Hathor-headed
handle inscribed for Amunet,
Priestess of Hathor
Middle Kingdom, Dynasty 12
Wood, bronze, silver, semi-precious
stones; 9 5/8" in height
From Thebes; CG 44052**

Mirrors were associated with various
goddesses, Hathor in particular.
A depiction of Hathor's head serves
as the terminal to which the disk
of this mirror is attached to its handle.
The funerary associations of mirrors
as offerings are clearly stated in several
temple texts, which implicitly state
that the mirrors are celestial orbs,
those with disks of gold and bronze
representing the sun, and those with
silver disks, as here, the moon (page
187). In versions of the primal
creation myth in which Hathor is the
principal figure, the narrative suggests
that Hathor, the genetrix of the
world, slept in the darkness of the
night and was awakened by the
dawn's early light; as a result creation
occurred. The very act of removing
the mirror from its box replicates the
rising of the sun from the swamp.
It is no accident, then, that Amunet,
the owner of this mirror, was a
priestess of Hathor. Darkness was also
compared to death, the light
dispelling it to rebirth. The moon,
too, was linked to rebirth because
it passed through monthly phases,
symbolizing birth, death, rebirth.
Those cycles could be associated with
Hathor, and other goddesses as well.
Objects, such as this mirror, were all
possessed of symbolic value because
the concept of art for art's sake did
not exist in ancient Egyptian
civilization; they were imbued with
symbolic overtones which transcended
their seemingly utilitarian functions.

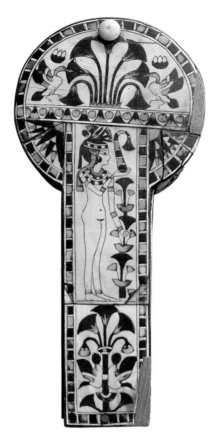

**Cover from a mirror case depicting
a female figure in a papyrus swamp
Third Intermediate Period, Dynasty 21
Stained wood and ivory
11 1/4" in height
From Thebes; CG 44101**

The close association between mirrors
and the swamp is well illustrated
by this mirror case. The scantily clad
female figure is surrounded by floral
forms, some of which she holds.
The ducks, in the lunette at the top
of the scene, are accompanied by
nests within which are unhatched
eggs. This is doubtless a reference
to Amun, the Great Cackler, as well
as to the primeval egg associated with
Geb, another genitor of life.
These references to creation are then
linked to references of resurrection
by virtue of the fact that the case and
its enclosed mirror, which is not
shown, was found within the mummy
bandages wrapped around the breast
of Queen Henettawy. Queen
Henettawy was one of the priestesses
of Amun, perhaps a chantress, whose
husband was Pinodjem I, high priest
of Amun at Thebes, and virtual ruler
of Upper Egypt at the time.

THE FUNERARY ARTS OF ANCIENT EGYPT

The tomb of Ti is one of the largest private tombs of the period at Sakkara; it is remarkable both for its exceptional state of preservation and for the care with which it has been restored. Its scenes, like those of most tombs, have been described as vignettes of private life, but their very appearance in a tomb suggests that they should be linked to funerary themes instead.

One of the most famous scenes in this tomb is that of Ti in a papyrus skiff, traveling upon the waters of a swamp. Not only is this scene a staple theme in the decoration of private tombs of all periods up to the end of the New Kingdom, but it also graphically links the interpretations suggested for the marsh scene on other objects (pages 154-159) inextricably to a funerary context. In these terms, Ti is likened to the sun itself, traversing the swamp of creation under the night sky until he is resurrected on the morrow, through analogy with the rising sun.

The swamp in ancient Egypt was filled with beasts of every description. Some, such as the hippopotamus and the crocodile, became associated with the forces of evil which threatened the nocturnal progress of the sun; they became visible obstacles over which the deceased had to triumph. The hippopotamus, in particular, was habitually shown in these scenes being hunted with harpoons.

More than genre scenes, these wall reliefs suggest in concrete terms the dangers which lie ahead on the metaphorical road to resurrection, and it is these dangers over which the deceased must triumph, if the aspired resurrection is to occur. Such concrete representations of these religious concepts are perfectly understandable when one recalls the hieroglyphic nature of ancient Egyptian art. That art, like the language in which the Egyptians expressed their religious beliefs, was rooted in signs of objects visible in the world around them. These signs, some 700-800 in number initially, were abstractions of things in the real world of the Egyptians. It is for this reason that the ancient Egyptians selected the Nile River and its fauna as the metaphor for the journey toward resurrection. It expressed, perhaps better than any other image, the concept of humanity's eternal quest for immortality.

Many people believe that the ancient Egyptians must have been preoccupied with death because they seemed to have expended so much effort and wealth on the construction, decoration, and furnishings of their tombs. Such an assessment, however, is far from the mark. In point of fact, the ancient Egyptians were not fixated with death. They were obsessed with life. As one attempts to get a handle on this obsession, consider, for a moment, how other cultures regard life after death. In many of those cultures, life after death is a paradise, completely different from life on earth, where the living is easy and the deceased is provided with those things which he or she may have lacked in life. Such a paradise might have streets paved of gold, or be replete with lush gardens gushing with cool, clear streams of fresh water. In general, then, such visions of aspired paradise in other cultures regard the environment of that blessed state as something quite different from life on earth, and very desirable. For the elite members of Egyptian society, paradise was their life on earth. They would not change it for the world. As a result, the scenes which fill the walls of their tombs are often characterized as depicting vignettes of daily life. Indeed, the elite Egyptians were apparently so content with their situation in life that they wished to take that life with them, and aspired to do so. And yet, like all peoples, they realized that their vision of paradise had to differ in some way from life on earth. Try as they might, the Egyptians could only quantify that difference by asserting that in paradise, in their version of the hereafter, the grain grew to be taller than it did in this world. Imagine that–the only difference between life on earth and life in the hereafter was the height of the grain! That difference alone speaks volumes about the ancient Egyptian attitude toward life, because life after death for the elite members of that society was basically a continuation of the privileged life they had led on earth.

As one surveys the preserved scenes in Egyptian tombs from all epochs, one becomes increasingly aware of the fact that the vignettes do not dwell upon themes of death. True, there are those scenes which depict the funerary procession and acts of mourning (page 168), typical of the grief which accompanies the loss of a loved one. But such scenes are statistically in the minority and are restricted to specific locations within the tomb. Elsewhere, scenes of the elite engaged in various kinds of activities associated with daily life predominate. These scenes have several levels of interpretation. On one level, their presence in the tomb is to insure the permanence of the deceased's station in life. Just as an individual may have been a high official and a chief priest in life, so in death he or she would symbolically retain that same status, and would continue to discharge the responsibilities of office in accordance with his or her monarch's directives. On another level, some of these seemingly daily life scenes were charged with symbolic value. Hunting and fishing in the marshes which figure so prominently in many scenes from tombs of the New Kingdom and are repeatedly represented on both cosmetic objects (pages 154 and 158-159) and even in some scenes apparently decorating palaces and temples, are replete either with resurrection symbolism linked to the renewed virility of Osiris or to the regenerative forces of Hathor. Such scenes, therefore, are not to be dismissed simply as manifestations of the ancient Egyptian love for their marshes and swamps.

In such contexts one constantly refers to the elite. The reason is simple. By their own admission, social anthropologists, in examining the archaeological record of ancient Egypt for evidence of the proverbial "man or woman on the street", candidly admit that such evidence is hard to find. The objects on view in this exhibition, as well as those filling the galleries of Egyptian collections worldwide, are to be associated with the elite because they were the members of Egyptian society who commanded the resources necessary for the construction, decoration, and appointment of their tombs (pages 160-161 and 166-167). Very little has survived from town sites. Since this is so, one should be cautious about interpreting any object found in a tomb as an object of daily life. These items were interred with the deceased members of the elite in order to fulfill specific ritual functions. The very fact that they were placed within the tomb to begin with should be reason enough for considering their funerary associations of paramount importance. Attempting to interpret such objects from a practical, functional point of view, although worthwhile, should be a secondary concern.

One example will suffice. The gold ewer from the Tanite tomb of Psusennes I (page 186) is not an elegant vessel used at a dinner party. An examination of the inscription, cold worked, reveals the presence of burrs, indicating that the craftsman responsible did not file the vessel down after he cut the text. This shows that the vessel was intentionally made for the tomb, and this is supported by the observation that the inscription calls Psusennes "the beloved of Osiris, lord of eternity." Furthermore, the shape of this particular vessel is often used in ceremonies in which incense and cool water are offered for the benefit of the deceased.

In like manner the presence of mirrors as funerary offerings (page 158) has often been regarded as evidence that the ancient Egyptians were preoccupied with cosmetics and personal appearance, and that they wished to be provided with such toiletries and their accompanying paraphernalia eternally. A careful reading of the inscriptions in which mirrors figure prominently suggest that the mirrors are in fact symbols of the celestial orbs, the sun and moon. Consequently their presence within the tomb is to insure the deceased of such orbs so that he or she might be resurrected through analogy with the rising sun at dawn or the waxing of the full moon after its monthly waning.

Among the most common objects in any burial are funerary figurines, often termed shabtis (pages 170 and 172-173), the ancient Egyptian name for which changed over time. The earliest such figurines gained in popularity during the course of the Middle Kingdom and continued to the very end of the Ptolemaic Period, to judge from a shabti inscribed for a priest of the god Ptah who is known to have served under the Macedonian Greek queen of Egypt, Cleopatra VII. Contrary to popular opinion, these figurines were not intended to wait hand and foot upon the deceased in the hereafter as if they were personal maids or butlers. On the contrary, the shabtis were required to perform specific agricultural tasks in the hereafter as surrogates for the deceased, man or woman, king or queen. Nevertheless, the personal maid/butler association with shabtis was so strong during the Roman Imperial Period, that this mistaken notion of the function of such figures survived the fall of ancient Egyptian civilization, and is the theme upon which the tale of the Sorcerer's Apprentice is based.

During the processes of mummification, the brain was removed and discarded, because the ancient Egyptians considered it of little consequence. Other internal organs were deemed worthy of preservation and these were often removed, preserved, and stored in four separate vessels, generally termed Canopic Jars (page 174-175). In time each of these jars was provided with a lid in the form of one of the Four Sons of Hor to whom the organ contained within was entrusted, and that organ was then likewise under the protection of a guardian goddess.

Before ending this brief survey of ancient Egyptian funerary arts, two very important considerations must be presented. The first is intended to demon-

The ancient Egyptians were not obsessed with death, but with life; they aspired to the perpetuation of that life in the hereafter. Funerary offerings, such as domestic items and shabtis, were buried with the deceased for their symbolic, more than their functional, value.

strate that the ancient Egyptians were not as materialistic as they appear to have been at first glance. The second suggests that however hard the elite members of that society tried, their efforts at obtaining immortality by the construction, decoration, and provisioning of a tomb were considered in some quarters to have been in vain, because as one will see presently, certain ancient Egyptian texts loudly proclaim that death is the ultimate end.

To state that the ancient Egyptians were not materialistic seems a curious claim to make insofar as the appointment of the elite tomb is concerned. How, one might ask, can it be suggested that the members of the ancient Egyptian elite were anything but materialistic, given the wealth of those tombs and their furnishings? The objection raised is typical of the way in which many individuals approach ancient Egyptian civilization. These individuals see the objects but almost never take into consideration the texts which the ancient Egyptians composed and which place their art and architecture into context. The funerary inscriptions and the spells which in the later periods were gathered into papyrus scrolls, and which a modern terms The Book of the Dead, but which the ancient Egyptians entitled The Book of Coming Forth by Day, are replete with moral and ethical concerns to which each and every member of Egyptian society was expected to adhere. No matter how gloriously designed and decorated and no matter how sumptuously appointed a tomb might be, its owner would not be guaranteed eternal life simply because he or she possessed a tomb.

Quite the contrary, the tomb owner was expected to demonstrate that he or she led a moral, ethically upright life on earth before being granted the privilege of eternal life. Proof of this assertion is provided by certain spells in The Book of Coming Forth by Day, as recorded in Chapters 30 and 125, and their variants. In the former chapter, the heart of the deceased is weighted against a feather of truth. A heart heavier than the feather indicates a life of turpitude. In the latter the deceased is obliged to make a "Declaration of Innocence" before the assessor gods in the hall of justice. The declaration takes the form of a negative confession, not unlike the Judaeo-Christian Ten Commandments which use the word "not" to indicate those activities from which a moral individual should refrain. The ancient Egyptian was required to assert, among other claims, that he or she had not killed, that he or she had not deprived the thirsty of water, the hungry of food, the naked of clothing. The declaration revolves around social issues and the deceased goes to great lengths to indicate that he or she has not acted in life in a socially reprehensible way. Such declarations clearly indicate that the ancient Egyptians were possessed of a social conscience, and as members of the elite were well aware of the plight of the less fortunate whose well-being appears to have been one of their paramount concerns. If the deceased was judged to have acted in a socially unacceptable manner, his or her heart would be cast by the gods into the mouth of Ammit, the great devourer who was represented as a formidable composite beast, part lion, part hippopotamus, part crocodile. And once Ammit had gobbled up the heart, the deceased was annihilated and ceased to exist forever and ever. No tomb, no matter how lavishly appointed, would redeem those who acted in a socially reprehensible manner.

This, then, is the lesson to be learned about the funerary arts of the ancient Egyptians. Resurrection into the afterlife could be easily achieved with a well-appointed tomb provided that the deceased had led a morally correct and ethically upright life.

Nevertheless, the ancient Egyptians seemed to be rather realistic about death. In many of the tombs, particularly those at Thebes which date to the New

The aspired resurrection into the afterlife was not guaranteed by wealth; funerary inscriptions reveal the emphasis that was placed upon the importance of a morally upright life.

From the time of the unification
of Egypt at the very beginning of the
dynastic period, the importance of
Sakkara as a cemetery and cult center
was never eclipsed. During the course
of the Late Period many high officials
elected to be buried here at Sakkara.
One of those was Psamtik, Chief of
Physicians. His tomb, sunk very deep
into the bedrock, is just to the south
of the Pyramid of Pharaoh Unas,
which was probably open and visited
by Psamtik and his contemporaries.
Impressed by the sarcophagus
chamber and the Pyramid Texts carved
into its walls, Psamtik commissioned
the craftsmen in his employ to erect
his own tomb and decorate its interior
chambers in imitation of those of
Pharaoh Unas, who had lived almost
two millennia before.
Such artistic quotations, termed
archaizing, reveal that the members
of the Egyptian elite did have a sense
of history; they recognized the
accomplishments of earlier
generations and appreciated the value
of older forms which they repeatedly
adapted for their own contemporary
needs. By means of such archaizing
many of the traditions of the elite
were preserved and passed on from
generation to generation.

Kingdom, among the so-called scenes of daily life one finds representations of corpulent individuals playing the harp with their eyes closed, a pose evocative of modern musicians in the throes of their musical expression. These vignettes are accompanied with hieroglyphic inscriptions which are traditionally called The Song of the Harper. The lyrics express a very hedonistic view of life; the harpist advocates eating, drinking, and being merry, and links that carpe diem motif to death which, the musician claims, is inevitable and final. There is no afterlife, or so he claims. This note of pessimism suggests yet another way for a modern to regard the funerary arts of the ancient Egyptians.

Relief from the Tomb of Ptahnefer, Scribe of the Treasury (detail)
New Kingdom, Dynasty 19
Sandstone; 44 3/4" in width
From Sakkara; 10/6/24/2
This scene in which the deceased is actually represented is frequently encountered in Egyptian tombs. The deceased is shown mummiform, attended by an Anubis-headed male figure. It is idle to speculate about whether this animal-headed figure is a priest in a mask or the god himself, because such a query arises out of a Western perception of visual images. Ancient Egyptian art was symbolic, not representative. In such a case, therefore, the Egyptians would have regarded the Anubis-headed figure symbolically as the god Anubis himself, metaphorically appearing to administer to the needs of the deceased's mummification. A priest, offering incense and cool water, is also shown in the center of the relief. The main inscription suggests why the Egyptian Book of the Dead should more correctly be termed The Book of Coming Forth by Day, and reads: *Go forth, Ptahnefer, Scribe of the Treasury, go forth! The sky lies open for thee. The earth lies open for thee. The trails to the Underworld likewise lie open for thee so that thou mayst go forth and enter in the company of Re and so that thou mayst walk about freely like the Masters of Eternity.*

Relief from the Tomb of Seyempetret, Head of the Goldsmiths, and of his wife, Neshet,
New Kingdom, Dynasty 19
Limestone; 18 1/2" in height
From Sakkara; JE 52542
This relief was purchased for the collections of the Egyptian Museum in Cairo from Mr. Maurice Nahman, a leading antiquarian in Cairo in the 1920s, by Professor Ludwig Keimer, who had a life-long interest in the flora of ancient Egypt. The relief shows the tomb owner and his wife, at the right, receiving offerings from a personified tree: *A prayer by the sycamore tree freely offered... I give you bread and cool water...* The link between word and image is clear. The sycamore, given a woman's head, shoulders, and arms, extends her hands, holding loaves of bread and ewers, to the deceased couple who cup their mouths with their own hands to catch the water and drink it. Perched on the register between these main figures are two human-headed, or ba birds, representing one of the forms which the deceased, Seyempetret and Neshet, might assume.
The tree is personified as an anonymous goddess, which in other instances is associated with such goddesses as Hathor and Isis, who provide nourishment by breast-feeding their children. Here the deceased are to enjoy eternal nourishment – bread and cool water – from the mother goddess.

Niche Stela with the God Osiris in honor of the Official Iritereru
Late Period, Dynasty 26
Painted limestone; 17 3/4" in height
From Abydos; CG 70028
The ancient Egyptians often identified in death with the god Osiris. That identification is visually suggested in art whenever pharaoh or a member of the elite is represented in the guise of Osiris, who is bearded and generally holds the crock and flail. He wears the atef-crown, the White Crown of Upper Egypt, to which are attached two feathers.
This stela is a rebus, or visual pun. The deceased, identified with Osiris, has been laid to rest within the tomb, compared to the recess in which the image of Osiris stands. Both aspire to resurrection on the morrow, through analogy with the rising sun. That wish is eloquently expressed by the scene in the lunette. The primeval hill from which the sun metaphorically rises is indicated as a U-shaped image, in reality the hieroglyph for "horizon," which represents a sand-covered mountain. Tombs, here the niche, are generally found underneath those mountains. The sun rising over the horizon is indicated by the sun disk itself, which is being worshipped by two baboons. In the wild, these mammals were observed warming themselves in the early rays of the sun, and screeching. The Egyptians interpreted that screeching as a hidden language, the secret speech of the baboons, offered as a prayer to the sun. The stela is therefore a rebus which visually demonstrates the processes of death and resurrection.

**Shabtis of the Lady Nesikhonsu,
as a laborer and as a foreman** (left)
**Third Intermediate Period, Dynasty 21
Faience; 7 1/4" average height
From Thebes; JE 26239 a & b**

Shabti of Pharaoh Amunemhat II
(page 172)
**New Kingdom, Dynasty 18
Unidentified black stone;
8 7/8" in height
From Thebes; CG 24201**

Shabti of Pharaoh Amunhotep II
(page 173)
**New kingdom, Dynasty 18
Alabaster; 8 7/8" in height
From Thebes; CG 24230**

Funerary figurines such as these first
appear as part of the funerary
equipment of the deceased during
the Middle Kingdom. Their name,
in the ancient Egyptian language,
changed over time, so that the word,
shabti, only represents an English
approximation of one of those
designations. Traditionally depicted as
male, not female, figures, such shabtis
were, nevertheless, interred with the
deceased regardless of their sex,
pharaoh or queen, man or woman;
they were meant to perform certain
tasks in the hereafter as specified in
Chapter 151 of some versions of The
Book of Going Forth by Day, which
is popularly termed The Book of the
Dead. There are numerous versions
and variations of this spell, one
of which is given here: *O shabti, if the
deceased is called upon to do any work
in the God's domain, while obstacles
have been erected against him or
her there, as a man to his duties, to the
irrigation of the fields, or to water the
banks, or to row sand of the east to the
west, I will do it. Here I am.* The work
described appears to be agricultural
in nature, and was apparently so
odious that the shabtis were intended
to serve as surrogates for the deceased
and perform the labor on his or her
behalf. Yet even the shabtis
metaphorically balked at such a
prospect, so that ideal sets contain
one shabti for every day of the ancient
Egyptian year, as well as a set of
overseers, who would make certain
they got to work on time. The
position of the right arm across the
chest on one of the shabtis of the
Lady Nesikhonsu (left) indicates that
that shabti is a foreman.

**A set of funerary amulets
Late Period, Dynasty 26
Faience; 2" average height
From Kantara; JE 88609**
This collection of 27 amulets was
discovered in 1942 in a sarcophagus
found by chance in the neighborhood
of the hospital at Kantara; they had
apparently been intended as part
of the funerary furnishing. The
whereabouts of the mummy and
a description of the sarcophagus
were not recorded.
The collection is, nevertheless,
important for several reasons.
To begin with, each of the amulets
is made of faience, a modern word
derived from the name of the Italian
city of Faenza, which was the center
of a ceramic industry producing
blue-green glazed ware. This ware
so resembled the ancient Egyptian
medium that the city's name, in
modified form, was given to it by
early European visitors to Egypt.
Faience, a composite material, is still
imperfectly understood. From ancient
inscriptions and texts, one learns
that faience was a material imbued
with symbolic value by the ancient
Egyptians themselves. They regarded
the sheen of its surfaces as a symbol
of the sun and imputed to the color
green qualities of rebirth, regeneration,
and the like, appropriated from the
ability of green plants to lie dormant,
symbolizing death, only to sprout
again, metaphorically being reborn.
The use of faience and the color
green imbues these amulets with
powerful properties, the aim of which
was to ensure the deceased of
aspired resurrection.
The amulets divide into several
typologies, some represented by more
than one example. This multiplication
symbolically reinforces the meaning
inherent in the repeated motifs.
These include the triad of Isis, her son
Hor, and her sister, Nephthys, who,
having aided the resurrection of
Osiris, can now assist with that of the
deceased. The scarabs are associated
with the sun; the djed pillars with
stability, hence the ability to remain
upright; and the wedjet eyes both
with the celestial spheres of the sun
and the moon as well as with
connotations of protection (page
187). There are in addition a host
of figurines of deities, each possessed
of special characteristics which are
useful to the deceased.

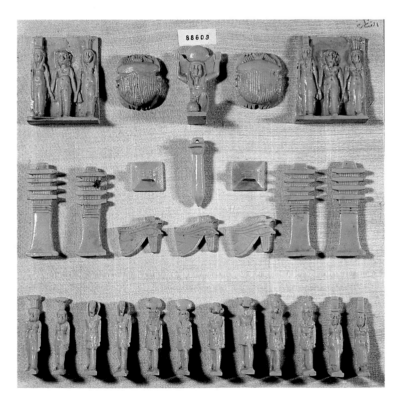

A set of Canopic Jars
Middle Kingdom, Dynasty 12
Painted alabaster; 14" in height
From Dashur; CG 4059-62
As early as the Old Kingdom,
the ancient Egyptians realized that
the internal organs, if left untreated
within the abdominal cavity, would
accelerate the putrefaction of the
body. As a result, these were removed
and placed into special containers,
modernly termed Canopic Jars. The
brain, considered to be of little value,
was removed and discarded. The
earliest of these Canopic Jars have flat
lids. As time passed, the shape of the
lid was transformed into an image
symbolically representing the
deceased, as here. At a still later date,
each Canopic Jar was provided with
a lid representing one of the Four
Sons of Hor. Elaborate rituals and
prayers were associated with these
four vessels, which were additionally
regarded as being under the
protection of four goddesses.

Bracelets and Broad Collar of
the Lady Ipiheresenebef (page 176)
Middle Kingdom, Dynasty 12
Faience of various colors;
approx. 11 1/2" in width (collar)
From Sakkara; JE 47899

Bracelets and Broad Collar
of Queen Itaweret (page 177)
Middle Kingdom, Dynasty 12
Gold, carnelian, turquoise,
green faience, lapis lazuli;
approx. 11" in width (collar)
From Dashur; 1/11/36/20
Both members of the elite
and members of pharaoh's court
commissioned similar jewelry as part
of their funerary equipment. The
difference in the materials employed
is an indication of the difference
in social status and, to some extent,
of wealth. The materials used for the
jewelry of Itaweret, like the faience
in that of Ipiheresenebef, are
symbolically charged. Gold was
associated with the flesh of the gods
of ancient Egypt. Carnelian, by virtue
of its red color, may have been
associated with the sun, although
the ancient Egyptians repeatedly
associated carnelian with evil.
The necklace of Itaweret is of
particular interest because it has
a counterpoise in order to balance the
necklace on the body when worn. Its
presence has been interpreted by some
to indicate that it was worn in life.

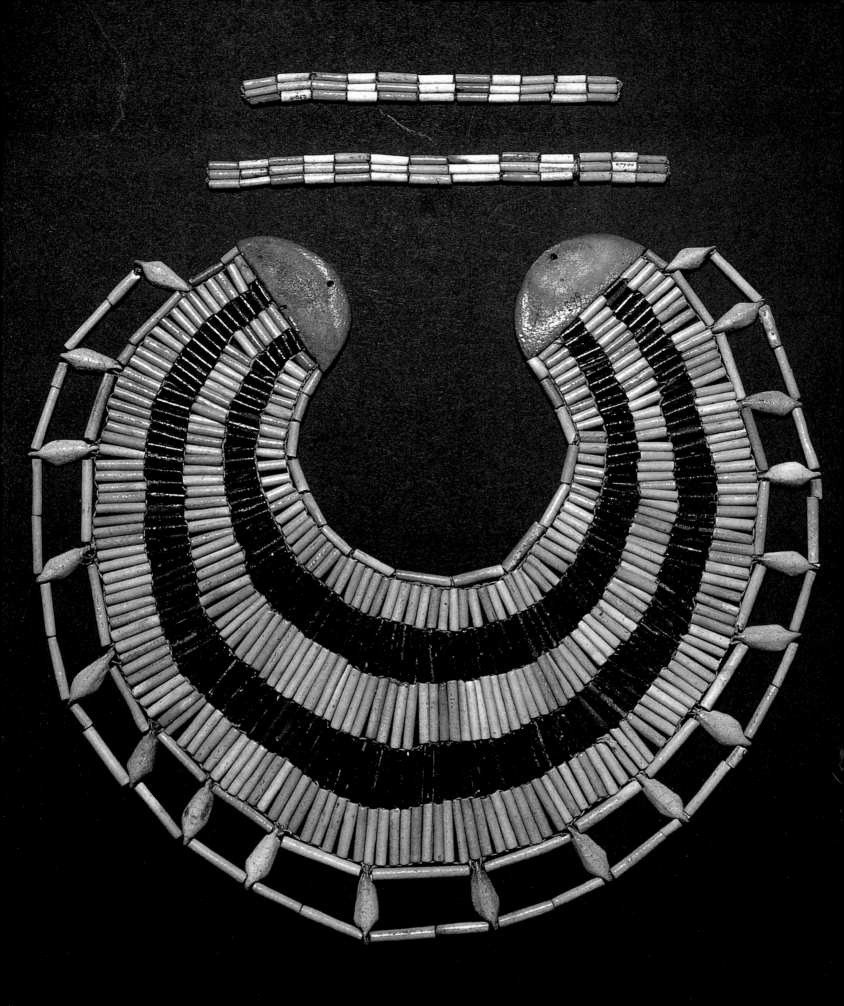

Funerary Mask of Wendjebaendjed
Third Intermediate Period, Dynasty 21
Gold with inlays; 8 1/8" in height
From Tanis; JE 87753
Spectacular events in Egyptian archaeology often occur suddenly, within days of the beginning of an excavation, as occurred when the Memphite tomb of Horemheb was discovered (pages 152-153). More often, however, such events are the result of season after season of painstakingly meticulous excavation and analysis, as happened in the case of the discovery of the royal tombs at Tanis, in the eastern Delta.
The Frenchman Pierre Montet began excavating at Tanis in 1929, firmly believing that the site was actually the famous city of Pi-Rameses mentioned at the beginning of Exodus. Eleven seasons later, in 1939, he hit pay dirt. It was not his intention to seek treasure; devoted archaeologists shun such pursuits. Montet was simply doing his job, methodically. He had surveyed the site and realized that the southern enclosure wall, which surrounded the precinct of the god Amun, was not parallel to the wall of the temple, as one expected it to be. That wall deviated and ran, instead, in a south-westerly direction. Such a departure troubled Montet, who realized that every such anomalous architectural feature could be explained in terms of the history of the site.
Late in February, 1939, he began his eleventh season at Tanis, and turned his attention to the space between the temple and the enclosure wall in an effort to explain that wall's deviation from its expected parallel orientation. Soon he chanced upon an unpretentiously small underground complex which had been erected in a helter-skelter fashion out of irregular blocks of stone, some of which, because they were inscribed, clearly revealed that they had been usurped from other structures and were reemployed here.
That underground complex, it now turns out, was the burial place of two pharaohs of Dynasty 21, three more pharaohs of Dynasty 22, one apparent co-regent, one prince, and two army commanders – nine burials, over half of which were royal!

As he continued to work during the course of that season, World War II erupted on September 1, 1939. The world's attention was now turned to more global, more immediate, and more important matters. By the time it had ended, Montet's discovery had become stale news; no one was interested in covering such an old story. And so, the discovery of the century, far more important in many, many ways than the discovery of the tomb of Tutankhamun, passed virtually unnoticed. Today, visitors to the Egyptian Museum in Cairo are attracted like flies to Gallery 3 on the second floor, where the more flashy jewelry of Tutankhamun is on view. Little do they realize that the east wall of that gallery is all that separates them from the fabulous Tanis Treasure, which is squeezed into a tiny room in Gallery 2. Even fewer still realize that the two dull gray anthropoid sarcophagi, of some considerable size, housed in wood and glass floor cases in Corridor 11 are actually made of silver and were recovered from Tanis as well.
The discovery of Tutankhamun's tomb did ignite the imagination of many and revived an interest in ancient Egypt. One wonders what the media, fanning the fires of ancient Egypt which many fuel, would have done had they had the opportunity to cover the spectacular discovery at Tanis in better times...
The presence of some of the wonderful objects from those royal tombs are included here, not only as an attempt to redress public opinion, but to demonstrate as well that ancient Egypt during the Third Intermediate Period was technologically advanced, particularly in the field of metallurgy (pages 144-147). And those advances were to serve as a catalyst among the artists of the emerging city-states of Greece, who adapted those methods and eventually realized their potential in ways never imagined by the Egyptians themselves.

The Goddess Isis on a necklace
for General Wendjebaendjed (overleaf)
Third Intermediate Period, Dynasty 21
Gold; 4" in height (Isis), **32" in length**
(chain); **From Tanis; JE 87716**
This gold figurine, attached to a gold chain of herring-bone design, was one of twelve statuettes found on the body of General Wendjebaendjed, the function of which was to protect him in the hereafter in much the same way as the collection of 27 faience amulets (page 171), associated with the sarcophagus, were intended to safe-guard their owner. The appearance of Isis in a funerary context is almost self-evident because she it was who almost single-handedly ministered to her slain husband and brought about his ultimate resurrection. Her presence on the mummy suggests that she would magically do the same for the general.
The figure of Isis wears a tightly-fitting sheath, armlets, bracelets, and a broad collar. Her large wig supports her attributes in the form of a cow's horns and sun disk. Although these are the insignia traditionally associated with Hathor, the figure is certainly Isis, as the inscription of that name on the base guarantees. During the course of the Third Intermediate Period, the cult of such goddesses, particularly Isis, gained in popularity until she eclipsed all other deities.

**Funerary Mask of
Pharaoh Psusennes I
Third Intermediate Period,
Dynasty 21
Gold with inlays of lapis lazuli
and glass; 18 1/8" in height
From Tanis; JE 85913**

**Pectoral of Pharaoh Psusennes I with
a winged scarab motif** (previous page)
**Third Intermediate Period, Dynasty 21
Gold, with red and green jasper, green
feldspar and glass, colored blue,
black, and red; 10" in width** (pectoral)
From Tanis; JE 85789
Four such pectorals, or chest
ornaments, were found on the body
of pharaoh Psusennes I. This example
is provided with a counterpoise in the
form of a lotus flower which was
intended to keep the pectoral poised
on the chest. The jewel was not worn
in life, because the back of the scarab,
which resembles a Japanese beetle, is
inscribed with a version of chapter 30
of The Book of Going Forth by Day.
This chapter, generally reserved for
so-called heart scarabs, insures the
deceased that his/her heart, regarded
as an individual's conscience,
will not testify against the deceased
in the Hall of Judgement in the
hereafter. It also specifies that such
amulets are to be made of green
stone, a recommendation followed
in this instance.
The motif of the scarab is based
on the observation of a dung beetle
rolling a ball of cow dung across
a pasture. For the ancient Egyptians,
this natural act provided the visual
metaphor which explained how the
sun moved across the heavens. It was
pushed by an invisible scarab.
Resurrection was sometimes explained
through analogy with the rising sun
(page 169). Through such analogies,
the hope was expressed that the king
might become united with the sun
god. This jewel is an eloquent
expression of that notion. The king,
who is identified in funerary contexts
with the sun, becomes the sun via
his name, which is enclosed within
the cartouche which the scarab pushes
because it has been intentionally
substituted in this context for the sun.
The circular attachment at the bottom
of the scarab is called a shen-sign,
itself a form of the cartouche, which
is used to symbolize all that which the
sun encircles. The cyclic nature of the
Egyptian cosmos is therefore visually
reaffirmed. The blues and greens are
charged with overtones of
rejuvenation and resurrection;
the gold refers to the flesh of the
gods and imbues the jewel with divine
connotations; and the reds may be
associated with the sun itself.
The jewel is wonderfully crafted
because the designs on the front were
repeated on the back.

**Finger stalls of the General
Wendjebaendjed** (pages 184-185)
**Third Intermediate Period, Dynasty 21
Gold; 3" average length
From Tanis; JE 87754**
Wendjebaendjed, doubtless for
meritorious service in his capacity
as general of the army, received the
singular distinction of being granted
a burial within the tomb of Pharaoh
Psusennes I. It was only in 1946,
some seven years after the excavations
of the royal tombs of Tanis had
begun, that his tomb was discovered
within the fourth chamber of the
tomb built for Psusennes I.
In order to guarantee the use
of hands and feet in the hereafter,
funerary practices often associated
gold, symbolizing the flesh of the
gods, with those parts of the body.
The transformation of the deceased
into a divine being and the
preservation of the digits themselves
doubtless motivated the funerary
priests to encase them in such gold
sleeves. Notice how each was
proportioned to correspond to the
actual differences in size between the
lengths of human fingers, and the
care that was lavished on the
depictions of their nails and cuticles.

**Ewer from the tomb of Pharaoh
Psusennes I, inscribed
for Pharaoh Ahmoses
Third Intermediate Period, Dynasty 21
Gold; 5 5/8" in height
From Tanis; JE 85865**

Among the treasures found in the
tomb of pharaoh Psusennes I at
Tanis was this remarkable ewer, used
in libation rituals which required
the cultic dispensing of liquids. The
vessel, crafted of two pieces of gold
which were then soldered together,
is inscribed in hieroglyphs in
the rectangular panel. Those signs
translate: *The good god, Ahmoses,
true of voice, beloved of Osiris, Lord
of Abydos.* The pharaoh named
is Ahmoses (pages 88-93) who was
in part responsible for driving the
Hyksos out of Egypt. Because recent
archaeological excavations suggest
that the Hyksos were resident at Tell
el Daba, which is very close to the
site of Tanis, Psusennes I must have
considered Ahmoses one of his
spiritual ancestors, with whom he may
have wished to commune in death.
The pristine condition of the ewer,
its similarity to other examples
of plate vessels found in the tombs
at Tanis, and the fact that the
hieroglyphs appear to have been cold
worked into the gold suggest that
this ewer was made expressly for the
burial of Psusennes I. It is unlikely,
therefore, to have been an heirloom
preserved from the time of Ahmoses.

**A pair of bracelets from the burial
of Pharaoh Sheshonk II
Third Intermediate Period, Dynasty 22
Gold, lapis lazuli, carnelian, white
faience (?); 3" in height
From Tanis; CG 52046-8**

Sources seem to indicate that
Osorkon I elevated his son, Sheshonk
II, to the position of co-regent,
but Sheshonk died within a year of his
accession. Despite the fact that these
rulers belonged to Dynasty 22,
the heirs of Sheshonk II apparently
ordered his interment within the
antechamber of the tomb of
Psusennes I, pharaoh of Dynasty 21.
The intact burial of Sheshonk II was
among the first uncovered by Montet
in 1939.

The design of the bracelets, each
crafted from two curved sections of
unequal length, is very contemporary
and relies upon the use of
interlocking, hollow tubes fastened
to each of the edges of two sections
comprising a single bracelet. A pin
is then slotted through each of the
sections where the tubes meet.
By means of such a simple device, the
bracelets could be put on and taken
off, by inserting or removing the pins.
These bracelets form a pair and were
intentionally designed to be worn
together. Their common motifs are
the sacred eye over a basket (page
171). These are actually two
hieroglyphs which can be translated,
All protection, an appropriate phrase
for bracelets which were found on

a king's body. The symbolism,
however, does not end there but
is extended to the eyes themselves.
A conscientious visitor will notice that
the two eyes actually represent one
left eye and one right eye, associated
with the moon and sun, respectively.
The levels of symbolism now become
multi-tiered. On the one level, the
left, or moon eye, was regarded as the
eye of Hor injured in his struggles
against Seth, his evil uncle. The right
eye is associated with the sun.
Sheshonk can find his way along the
paths of the underworld because
he is guided by divine eyes which see.
On another level, he is provided with
celestial orbs, the sun and the moon
themselves, which, as one has seen
in the discussions of mirrors, are
themselves symbols of resurrection
(page 158). The pluralistic approach
to motifs, so characteristic of ancient
Egyptian intellectual discourse, is
clearly evident in these bracelets. The
seeming simplicity of their decoration
should not obscure the profundity
of their symbolic value.

Previous page
The Palace of Pharaoh Apries
Late Period, Dynasty 26, Memphis
It is hard to imagine a more picturesque setting for a palace than this, perched high atop a hill overlooking both the ancient city of Memphis and, in the distance, the necropolis of Sakkara in which the Step Pyramid of Djoser of Dynasty 3 appears so prominently (pages 40-41). In antiquity, the palace must have presented an awe-inspiring sight; the size of the preserved column capitals suggest that it towered high above the hill on which it was built. The choice of this hill and its alignment with the Step Pyramid was not accidental. One has already seen how members of the elite of this period visited, admired, and modelled their own tombs on those of their distant forefathers (pages 166-167). This admiration for the past even extended to the pharaohs of Dynasty 26. They ordered their craftsmen down into the burial shafts of the Step Pyramid of Djoser and there, on the reliefs created during Dynasty 3, they superimposed their own network of gridlines so that they could imitate more accurately this Old Kingdom style of art. Apries was certainly aware of these activities, and he may very well have thought, as he beheld the Step Pyramid of Djoser in the distance, that he was that pharaoh's legitimate successor. The point may not have been lost on his contemporaries, when one recalls that Apries eventually lost both his throne and his life because of his excessive reliance upon Greek mercenaries (pages 190-195). The column capitals, many inscribed with the name of Apries, are of a developed form of the composite floral type encountered earlier during Dynasty 20.

In order to understand the origins of the Late Period, one must pay some attention to the events in Nubia. During the course of the New Kingdom, doubtless as a result of the military campaigns of such pharaohs as Tuthmoses III, the Kushites gradually embraced many aspects of ancient Egypt's culture, not the least important of which was their devotion to Amun. The onslaught of the Sea Peoples during the course of Dynasty 20 was so overwhelming that the Egyptian military detachments in Kush were ordered to return to Egypt to address those invasions. The resulting political vicissitudes eventually witnessed the break up of Egypt and the emergence of the Third Intermediate Period, at which time Egypt was again divided into two separate political spheres. As a result of these events, the Blacks of Kush were no longer under the domination of the Egyptians. They developed an independent kingdom far to the south of Aswan in the region of the Fourth Cataract. There they devoted themselves almost exclusively to the worship of the god Amun, whose cult in the region had earlier been encouraged by such warrior pharaohs as Tuthmoses III.

In time the Kushites recognized the political division which existed in Egypt. They reasoned that they themselves, as regents of the god Amun on earth, might remedy the situation by invading that land, uniting the country, and restoring the central authority of pharaoh and the prestige of Amun. They regarded their conquest of Egypt, then, not as a simple military campaign, but rather as a holy war, the objective of which was to punish those who had strayed from the path of Amun. Their leader was Piankhy, sometimes called Piye, and the accounts of his campaigns against Egypt have been recorded in a series of inscribed stelae which were discovered late in the last century in Kush and are now in the collections of the Egyptian Museum in Cairo. One of Piankhy's exhortations to his troops reads as follows: *Enter combat, engage in battle... do not attack by night in the manner of draughts-playing; fight when one can see... form your battle line, and know that Amun is the god who sent us...* In time, Thebes fell. The independent princes of Lower Egypt placed aside their petty jealousies in order to join forces in an effort to challenge the Kushite presence in their land. Still the Kushite forces of Piankhy pressed ever northward. Town after town surrendered, rather than risk attack. One such prince explained his resistance to Piankhy, whom he finally accepts as king, in the following, glowing terms: *Hail to you, Hor, mighty king, Bull attacking bulls! The netherworld seized me, I foundered in darkness... [but] you drove the darkness from me! As the god Horakhty is immortal, so, too, are you immortal, O King of Upper and Lower Egypt, Piankhy living forever!* The campaigns continued until Piankhy had vanquished most of his enemies, thereby gaining control of almost the entire country. There were some petty princes who still held out, and pockets of local resistance to Kushite rule, but these were relegated to the Delta.

At Thebes, the Kushites presented themselves as the legitimate pharaohs of Egypt (page 148). They erected numerous monuments in honor of Amun and enrolled their daughters as Divine Wives of Amun (page 151), perpetuating an important office which had begun in the early part of Dynasty 18. As advocates of Amun, the Kushites seem to have run into almost no resistance from the Theban elite, and marriages between members of that elite and the Kushites appear to have been quite common at the time.

The semblance of order which the Kushite presence had brought to Egypt was soon shattered by the Assyrians, intent on conquering Egypt and incorporating it into their ever-expanding empire. The Assyrian assault upon that land was launched by the Assyrian king, Esarhaddon, whose rival was the Kushite pharaoh Taharka. The Assyrian forces finally captured the city of Memphis, forcing Taharka to seek refuge in the south. Esarhaddon was succeeded by Ashurbanipal who realized that there was resistance to Kushite rule in Egypt, particularly among the Delta princes. He therefore marched against Egypt, but enlisted the aid of the princes of the Delta city of Sais as his collaborators by appointing them administrators of the land.

The forces of Ashurbanipal then returned to Egypt, routing the Kushite Tanwetamani, who had become pharaoh following the death of Taharka. They pressed on to Thebes, which some historians maintain was actually sacked by the Assyrians. Tanwetamani fled to the safety of his Kushite kingdom far to the south. The expulsion of the Kushites left the Delta princes, established by the Assyrians, as the virtual rulers of the land. When troubles at home aborted further attempts on the part of the Assyrians to exploit the situation in Egypt, Psamtik I, prince of Sais, declared himself pharaoh of Egypt. Nevertheless, he still had to contend with the strong Kushite religious presence at Thebes.

The mingling of the Kushite religious authorities, particularly those associated with the divine wives of Amun, with the Egyptian elite attached to the cult of Amun at Thebes was so strong that Psamtik I realized that military action against the city would be of little avail. As a result, he dispatched an embassy to Thebes, charged with negotiating the peaceful transfer of power. This was effected by the legal adoption of Nitocris, the daughter of Psamtik I, and her enrollment into the office of divine wife of Amun by the then reigning Kushite divine wife of Amun. This solution permitted the Kushite women to remain in that office until their natural deaths, whereupon Nitocris would assume the office. By such a stratagem the religious authority of the Theban cult of Amun was peacefully transferred from the Kushites to the Saites, as the kings of Dynasty 26 are called. This manoeuvre, while peaceful, did little to erode the power of the Theban elite, whose influence was to continue to grow, and whose opposition to all foreigners was to ensure the maintenance of pharaonic traditions well into the Roman Imperial Period.

The Saite Period marks a turning point in Egyptian history, because the Egyptians were now drawn into the political arena of the Greeks, whose services as mercenaries the Egyptians had come to rely upon. So, for example, during the reign of Psamtik II, the Egyptians decided to dispatch a punitive campaign against the Kushites, and that detachment was led by Greek mercenaries who left a mention of their exploits as a graffito on the foot of one of the colossal statues of Rameses II at Abu Simbel. The events of that campaign were recorded by the Saites as well: ...*The Nubians of every hill country rose up against him [Psamtik II], their hearts full of rage against him. His attack took place... the arrows did not sway from piercing them... One waded in their blood as in water. Not one bound pair escaped of the 4,200 captives. A successful deed has been done.* The subject of those inscriptions became the source for the story line in Verdi's opera *Aïda*.

As a result of such contacts, the Greeks may well have been exposed to a common type of Egyptian statuary which depicts the male figure striding forth with the left leg advanced (pages 50-51). Such a type doubtless influenced the development of the so-called kouros, or nude male figure in Greece, and recent scholarship suggests that the claw chisel, a technological innovation which contributed to the development of marble sculpture in Greece, was likewise introduced to the Greeks by the Egyptians.

Aware of the presence of the Kushites, acknowledging the dangers presented by oriental powers from abroad, and realizing the ever-increasing role of the Greeks in their own society, the members of the Egyptian elite attempted to ensure their advantaged position. One of the means to achieve this goal was the introduction of a very cursive form of the hieroglyphs, termed Demotic, which might be compared to modern short-hand. This script is very difficult for a modern to master, and anciently ensured that the number of Egyptians literate in this new script would be very limited indeed.

The Saites continued the policy of the Kushites regarding Egypt's illustrious past. The art as well as the inscriptions and literature of the period either repeatedly evoke earlier models or habitually imitate older forms. As a result, some scholars would go so far as to term the culture of Dynasty 26 the Saite Renaissance.

The Greek mercenary presence in Egypt continued to increase during the course of the sixth century B.C. and led to disastrous results for the Saite pharaoh Apries (pages 188-189). Relying on these mercenaries, his forces suffered such a humiliating defeat that an armed insurrection ensued when the Egyptian army engaged the mercenaries in battle. Apries was killed in the engagement, and he was followed as pharaoh by Amasis, who tried to contain the influence of these mercenaries whose presence was increasingly resented by the native Egyptian elite. Despite the waves of nationalism and anti-mercenary sentiments which caused the death of Apries, the Egyptians were drawn ever more tightly into the affairs of the Greeks as Dynasty 26 drew to a close. That involvement was due to their common enemy – the Persians.

In 525 B.C. the Persian army led by Cambyses, king of kings, invaded Egypt which was then immediately converted into a satrapy, or province (termed, for convenience, Dynasty 27) of the expanding Persian empire. The Persians, like the Hyksos before them, realized that it was to their advantage to enlist the collaboration of members of the Egyptian elite in the administration of the land. One such collaborator was the official Wedjehoresnet, who records his participation in these events: ...*Cambyses came to Egypt... he had conquered this land in its entirety... [he] assigned to me the office of chief physician. He made me live at his side as companion and administrator of the palace. I composed his titular naming... his majesty commanded [me] to cleanse the temple of the goddess Neith at Sais and to return all of its personnel to it...*

The tit-for-tat arrangement between foreigners and members of the Egyptian elite are here clearly articulated. Cambyses so trusts Wedjehoresnet that he becomes the Persian's official physician. On this personal level, Wedjehoresnet then shows Cambyses how to be pharaoh, by developing his name and titles in hieroglyphs. In return for such cooperation, Cambyses appoints Wedjehoresnet to the rank of administrator, and in such a capacity the Egyptian collaborator can perpetuate the advantages enjoyed in life by his associates because he convinces Cambyses of the desirability of refurbishing the famous cult temple of Neith, patron goddess of the former kings of Dynasty 26, at Sais. This act provides a number of well paying jobs for Wedjehoresnet's cronies, since Cambyses agrees to allow the temple's personnel to return to their hereditary positions. Such texts do much to restore the tarnished reputation imputed to the character of Cambyses by later generations, who regarded his administration of Egypt as utterly evil and sacrilegious. Wishing to appear devoted to the deities of the land, Cambyses even attempted to travel across the Libyan desert to reach a famed oracle of the god Amun. He never made it, because his entire army was killed en route, buried alive as a result of a massive sandstorm. Cambyses escaped, and was eventually succeeded by Darius the Great.

With the Persian invasion in 525 B.C., Egypt became a province of the Persian empire, but the Egyptian elite continued, through collaboration, to hold on to positions of power.

As if history were indeed repeating itself, turmoil within the heartland of the Persian Empire, like that at the Assyrian court earlier, caused the Persians to abandon Egypt. The removal of foreign authority encouraged competing local elites to vie with one another for control of the land. A series of contemporary, local dynasties, the 28th and 29th, then emerged. Both were ephemeral, yet each realized the possibility that the Persians might once more return to Egypt. And return they did, but their initial attempts at reconquest were successfully thwarted by the Egyptians.

The Persians again returned in 380 B.C., at a time when Nectanebo I had consolidated the political power of the country into his own hands. Despite the Persian advance as far as the city of Memphis, Nectanebo I was able to defeat them, and in so doing became the first pharaoh of Dynasty 30, which, as it turned out, was the last dynasty of ancient Egypt ruled by members of its own elite. The pharaohs of Dynasty 30 were energetic builders, either erecting new temples or refurbishing older ones throughout the length and breadth of the land. They fostered the worship of many deities, but perhaps none was more esteemed than Isis. The popularity of that goddess throughout the Greek and Roman world can be directly attributed to the honored place Isis enjoyed under the kings of this dynasty (page 180).

The last native king of Egypt, Nectanebo II, continued his family's devotion to the deities of the land. By one reckoning, his name appears on monuments at well over 100 different sites, rivaling, perhaps, the proclivities of Rameses II in that regard. Although his interests were varied, he was predisposed to the animal cults of Egypt, a phenomenon which deserves special comment. The ancient Egyptians, unlike other people, did not venerate each and every animal of a species. Instead, by means of a very selected and strictly regulated process, the priests of any given cult would scour the land in search of one animal–a cow, a bull, a hawk, a hare, a fish, or any other beast–whose physical markings matched a predetermined description. Once found, that animal was considered to be a manifestation of the deity with which it was associated, and it was kept in a special precinct. When it died of natural causes, this animal was reverentially mummified with all the accompanying rituals, bandages, and amulets, and piously interred in a tomb within a special cemetery reserved exclusively for these beasts. The cavernous vaults of the Apis Bulls beneath the sands of Sakkara are, perhaps, the best known of these sepulchers. The process was then repeated to identify a successor.

On the other hand, other animals, particularly cats, ibises, and baboons, were raised on special farms. When the festivals of the deities associated with these animals approached, special priests would cull the collections, selecting those specimens which they would then ritually murder and mummify. Thousands upon thousands of such animal mummies have been found at places like Sakkara, to the south of modern Cairo, and at Tuna al Gebel in Middle Egypt. Forensic examination of numerous cat mummies from Bubastis in the Nile Delta reveal that the cats were generally less than two years old at the time of their deaths and that the cause of those deaths was, in almost every case, an intentionally broken neck. Several of the mummies examined further reveal that they were not made of entire cats, but were rather composed of parts of different animals into which occasionally stray material, such as wood or other substances, were added. Whereas this practice appears to be somewhat uncivilized and out of character with modern perceptions of ancient Egyptian civilization, the ritual killing of such animals was, in fact, well within the traditions of ancient Egyptian religious beliefs. Just as Osiris was murdered by his

For a time the Persian threat was resisted. Nectanebo II of Dynasty 30 became the last native Egyptian to rule the country until General Abd-al Nasser almost 2000 years later.

Statue of the God Osiris, enthroned
Late Period, Dynasty 26
Graywacke; 15" in height
From Giza; CG 38367

This enthroned image of Osiris
is perfectly preserved, having been
excavated at Giza, where the cult
of the goddess Isis and Osiris enjoyed
renewed popularity during the course
of the Late Period. The god, as is to
be expected, wears a garment which
envelops his body and completely
covers his legs and feet. Such a
garment may be a reference to the
all-enveloping mummy bandages.
He holds as attributes a crock
and flail, and wears the atef-crown,
a combination of the white crown
flanked by two ostrich feathers.
A uraeus and false beard complete
his costume.

The mat finish which characterizes
the surfaces of this statue is a hallmark
of the art of Dynasty 26 and may be
a conscious imitation of the same
kind of finish found on statues of
Dynasty 4. Because of the tendency
of the craftsmen to base the faces
of the images of deities on those
of the reigning pharaohs, this image
of Osiris may be regarded as
exhibiting the idealizing features
of pharaohs of the second half of
Dynasty 26.

evil brother Seth and later resurrected for the benefit of the living, so, too, could such ritually slaughtered animals be of like benefit. Their resulting mummies were sold to pilgrims who would deposit the animal mummies in special cemeteries as either " please" or "thank you" offerings– "please grant my prayer", or "thank you for having granted my prayer". Such practices, already developed earlier, became a fixture of the religious climate in Egypt during Dynasty 30 and continued unabated well into the Roman and early Christian periods.

Despite the piety of such pharaohs of Dynasty 30, and the initial military successes they had enjoyed against the Persians, the independence of Egypt was short-lived, because this dynasty came to an end in 342 B.C. with the return of the Persians, led by Artaxerxes III. Nectanebo II valiantly attempted to defend his realm, but in the end he was put to flight and sought refuge among the Kushites. His fate remains unknown, and his empty sarcophagus, discovered in the eighteenth century in a mosque in Alexandria where it had been converted into use as a fountain, is now in the collections of the British Museum in London.

The Persian conquest of the land reestablished Egypt as a satrapy, governed by members of the elite in cooperation with the Persian king. Nevertheless, that conquest was short-lived, because of the appearance on the historical stage of Alexander the Great. Whereas it is not the aim here to outline his spectacular rise to power and the devastating alacrity with which his armies decimated the Persian foe, one must devote a few words to this Macedonian Greek conqueror because of his special, and very intimate, relationship with Egypt.

Of all the lands subdued by Alexander the Great, none save Egypt fell into his lap without so much as an arrow having been shot. The data available suggests that during his siege of Tyre and his subsequent march down the Syria-Palestine littoral, Alexander dispatched agents to Egypt who managed to obtain an agreement whereby the Persian governor and his staff, with the full cooperation of the Egyptian elite, would surrender Egypt to Alexander without a fight in exchange for their continuance in office. Alexander then marched into the country and was greeted by the Egyptians as a liberator who had freed them from the Persian yoke. Good to his word, those in power remained there. Their number even included blood relatives of Nectanebo II, the last native pharaoh of Egypt. That these members of that royal family could still enjoy such advantaged positions in society is yet again demonstration of just how resilient and pragmatic the members of the Egyptian elite continued to be.

In Egypt for less than six months, from the winter of 332 B.C. until the spring of the following year, Alexander accomplished three things, but their chronological order is disputed. It is certain that he performed ceremonies at Memphis in honor of the country's deities, but he was certainly not crowned pharaoh at that time, as some have erroneously asserted. He also traveled to the extreme western edge of the Nile Delta and there, along the coast, decided that the small fishing village of Rhacotis would make for a fine port. He ordered the enlargement of that village and renamed it in his honor. From that moment on, Alexandria was to become one of the most important cosmopolitan cities of the ancient world.

Finally, Alexander the Great, in an effort to out-do Cambyses, undertook the long, arduous march across the Libyan desert to the Siwa Oasis where he consulted the oracle of Amun. And although volumes have been written about this particular episode of his life, very little is known about what actually transpired there. One thing, however, is certain. Alexander the Great formed a very intense personal bond with the god Amun. He left Egypt, never to return alive, but was buried there by the Ptolemies who are the subject of the next chapter.

The personality of Alexander the Great was such, that his reputation continued to increase at an exponential rate after his death. So inextricably linked to Egypt and to Amun had Alexander the Great become that later generations of ancient Egyptians concocted the legend that the real father of Alexander the Great was none other than the state god Amun himself. This tale recounts how pharaoh Nectanebo II, fleeing Egypt before the invading armies of Persia, made his way to the Macedonian Greek court. There he was introduced to Olympias, and via a stratagem, effected the union between Amun and Olympias which resulted in her pregnancy. The child of that union was Alexander the Great.

The final conquest of Egypt by the Persians under Artaxerxes III was short-lived. In 332 B.C. Egypt fell to Alexander the Great without a battle; 300 years of Greek rule began.

Block statue of Hor, Prophet of the God Montu
Late Period, Dynasty 26
Graywacke; 20" in height
From Thebes; JE 37150

The dating of this statue is problematic because some scholars have not recognized that the date of the career of Hor, the individual commemorated, and the date at which the statue was commissioned and sculpted, are not the same. The inscriptions clearly reveal this temporal difference.

The titles which Hor holds are those which can be associated with the Kushite kings of Dynasty 25, during which time Hor must have exercised his obligations as prophet of the god Montu. However, the inscription on the base between the feet clearly states the following: *[This statue] was made by the elder son of his elder son, Hor...* The grandson, Hor, who made the statue in honor of his grandfather, after whom he was named, lived two generations after his grandfather. If one assumes, as some have, that the grandfather lived during the reign of Taharka, then Hor the grandson would have lived around the beginning of the Saite Period of Dynasty 26. It is to that period, then, that this statue is assigned.

Hor the grandfather is represented in a block statue. The rear of the base is raised, perhaps to indicate the presence of a cushion, which is clearly represented as such on other examples. His arms are folded over and rest on his knees. His hands hold what are termed emblematic staves, but which are probably to be interpreted as folded bolts of cloth. He wears a short beard, and a kilt which is held in place by a belt. That belt is of interest because it is one of the rare representations of a belt in Egyptian art which is inscribed with hieroglyphs along its entire visible length. His hair is arranged as a series of delicate locks.

The statue was found in the Luxor Cachette (pages 108-109), suggesting that it was originally placed in the precinct to share in the offering presented to Amun.

Previous page
Temple of the God Ptah
Late Period/Ptolemaic Period
Karnak

The Temple of Ptah at Karnak was originally erected under Tuthmoses III. It was refurbished in part under the Kushite pharaoh, Shabako (page 148), extensively remodelled during the second half of the Ptolemaic Period, and repaired under the Roman Emperor Tiberius.
The temple is characterized by its long approach, dominated by no less than six gates, the dimensions of which successively decrease as one approaches the sanctuary proper. Their design is intended to correspond to the proportional rise in floor level and decrease in ceiling height that one encounters when entering the space of the temple proper.
The temple is dedicated to Ptah as the principal god, as well as to members of his divine family and entourage. During the Late Period, particularly at Memphis, the reputation of Imhotep increased so greatly that he was considered to be a son of Ptah. It is for this reason that Imhotep, the god, is venerated in the temple as well. Extracts of the hymn to Ptah inscribed in hieroglyphs on the temple walls reveal how much his reputation had increased with the passing of time (pages 42-47).
Hail to you, o kind-hearted god,
Imhotep, the son of Ptah. Come to your
house, your temple in Thebes, so that
its people can joyously behold you...
Men applaud you, Women worship you,
One and all exalt your kindness.
For you heal them, You revive them...

THE PTOLEMAIC PERIOD

The death of Alexander the Great at Babylon on the banks of the Euphrates River in June of 323 B.C. threw his general staff into confusion because he had not indicated which of them would be his successor. While the generals schemed and plotted to gain possession of the empire of Alexander the Great, it was decided that his half brother, Philip Arrhidaeus by name, should be charged with overseeing the funeral arrangements. The body of Alexander the Great was mummified, in accordance with pharaonic traditions, and laid in state at Babylon, while the elaborate hearse and related ceremonies were planned, a series of activities that took at least two years to complete. In the end, the great funerary procession departed from Babylon with the intention of passing through all of Alexander's conquered lands en route to Macedonia in Greece, where the body of the general was supposed to be buried.

Along the way, the cortege was intercepted by Ptolemy, son of Lagos, a Macedonian Greek, somewhat older than Alexander the Great, who had been one of his most trusted inner staff members. In a bold action, he literally kidnapped the body of Alexander the Great by diverting the cortege from its scheduled route and beating a hasty retreat to Egypt. Once within the borders of that country, Ptolemy, son of Lagos, ordered the burial of Alexander the Great in Sakkara, not far from Memphis where Alexander in life had paid homage to the deities of Egypt. As if possessed of a talisman in the form of the mummified remains of the great leader, Ptolemy, son of Lagos, with the cooperation of the Egyptian elite, provisioned his army and secured the borders of Egypt against the Diadochs, as the successors of Alexander the Great are called. In 305 B.C. he took the unprecedented step of declaring himself pharaoh of Egypt, and thereby inaugurated a dynasty, named the Ptolemaic in his honor, whose members were to rule Egypt for about three centuries as Macedonian Greek kings.

The history of Egypt during those three centuries is a very complex one indeed. Egypt appears to have been characterized as two societies, separate and unequal. The Egyptian elite realized that their interests were best served by aligning themselves with the Ptolemies who were ruling from Alexandria. Whereas it is true that the Egyptians were not warmly received at the Alexandrian court of the Ptolemies, they themselves let it be known that the Ptolemies, and the Greeks in general, were not welcome in their local enclaves and temples. One reads prohibitions, written in hieroglyphs, over the entrances of Egyptian temples erected during this period, such as this: *Let no Greek, or other foreigner, tread across the threshold of this sacred area...* Temples continued to be built in pharaonic style and decorated with scenes and accompanying inscriptions which eschewed all influences from the Classical world.

So resistant were the native Egyptians to the Ptolemies that, as the Ptolemaic Period progressed, numerous revolts erupted, led by the members of the elite who attempted to become masters of their own fate. One such famous revolt occurred at Thebes, where , of course, the local elite, tied to the cult of Amun, had been entrenched since the time of the beginning of Dynasty 18. It is worth recalling the wisdom of Psamtik I, who sensibly gained the cooperation of the local elite, not by force of arms, but by arranging for the adoption of his daughter and her enrollment into the ranks of the divine wives of Amun (page 191).

Around 200 B.C. the Theban elite proclaimed its independence from Alexandria and rallied around two successive native Egyptians who were regarded as the legitimate pharaohs of the land. The famous decree on the Rosetta Stone, now in the collections of the British Museum in London, is dated to 196 B.C., during the reign of Ptolemy V Epiphanes, and is actually an official decree promulgated at the end of that revolt. It grants major concessions on the part of the Ptolemies in Alexandria to the native Egyptian elite and offers them enhanced benefits if only they would return the land to order.

Such revolts continued to characterize Egyptian society for the next century. Some were quelled only after bloody conflict, but the proliferation of decrees of amnesty issued by one Ptolemy after another reveals how serious a threat to their reigns such revolts were. The Ptolemies were always willing to address the grievances of the elite and grant them concessions in exchange for their cooperation with the regime.

It is within this context, then, that one can understand how the members of the Egyptian elite, ensconced within the confines of their temples, were able to maintain their millennia-old traditions. It has often been remarked that their introspection and avoidance of all things foreign enabled them to increase some tenfold the number of hieroglyphs at their disposal to between 7,000-8,000 individual signs. These they then composed into the most profound religious expressions ever penned in ancient Egypt. Champollion's decipherment of the hieroglyphs is all the more remarkable when one considers that the text of the Rosetta Stone, mentioned above, was written using many of these signs!

The Macedonian Greeks, on the other hand, were quick to realize the importance of Alexandria. Under the direction of Ptolemy II Philadelphos, the city grew by leaps and bounds. The famous lighthouse, or Pharos, at Alexandria was erected and soon was numbered among the Seven Wonders of the Ancient World. Alexandria became the most important port in the Mediterranean Sea, and the Ptolemies grew rich from the tariffs and taxes levied on luxury goods passing into and out of the city, as well as from the profits gained from many of the state-owned monopolies.

The great palace of the Ptolemies contained many dependencies, one of which was the Museion, an ancient equivalent of a modern think-tank, where the most learned men of the day, salaried and cared for by the state, devoted their attention to scholarly matters both humanistic and scientific. The great literary figures of the day came here to write while others served as librarians. Those engaged in the pure sciences also found a ready welcome in the Museion. Among them was Eratosthenes who calculated the circumference of the earth with amazing accuracy, and the physicians attached both to the Museion and to the cult of Asclepius on the Greek island of Cos, also a Ptolemaic possession, who explored the physiology of the human body as no physicians had done before.

In honor of his father, Ptolemy II Philadelphos erected a glorious tomb within the city of Alexandria, and there interred his parents and his wife. He also ordered the removal of the body of Alexander the Great from Sakkara and its reinterrment in this family mausoleum. Ptolemy IV Philopator, somewhat later, reorganized the royal burials and reinterred his ancestors as well as Alexander the Great in yet another memorial whose location, admittedly still not identified, remained nevertheless within the city of Alexandria. Despite recent claims to the contrary, the mummy of Alexander the Great remained within that city, and there it was viewed by a host of luminaries, including several later Roman emperors.

The kingdom of the Ptolemies continued to expand and reached the height of its power and prestige during the reign of Ptolemy III Euergetes. Soon, thereafter, the balance of power in the Eastern Mediterranean began to shift as the Seleucid empire, again founded by one of the Diadochs, or successors of Alexander the Great, began to rival Ptolemaic Egypt for supremacy of the region. As these two powers squared off against one another, a third force was rising in the west–Rome, whose meteoric rise from a simple city state had quickly caused her citizens to be masters of all of Italy. Their stunning defeat of

Inscriptions on the Rosetta Stone bear witness to the Egyptian revolts against Greek rule. The elite continued to cling to their ancient traditions.

Under the Ptolemies, Alexandria became a major Mediterranean port; its Pharos, or lighthouse, was one of the Seven Wonders of the Ancient World.

the Carthaginians as a result of the Punic Wars effectively made Rome mistress of the Western Mediterranean, with the result that she turned her attention to the Greek lands of the East. The second century B.C. ended with Rome's conquest of most of Greece and what is now modern Turkey. In time, Syria, too, fell into her grasp.

And so it happened that by the time of the first century B.C. there were only two superpowers left in the world – Rome and Egypt. The rulers of both aspired to world domination, although their means differed. It is only within this context that the career of Cleopatra VII can be presented.

Almost no woman of the ancient world has been the theme of so much speculation and the subject of so many Hollywood movies, operas, plays, novels, cartoons, and the like. Why is the West so fascinated with, and attracted by, Cleopatra the Great? The answer is difficult because of the complexities of the issues involved. One should, therefore, recount her biography, not in the way it has been misrepresented by the Romans and certain literary figures of the West, but by using the evidence preserved from ancient Egypt, which until just recently has been virtually ignored by most scholars.

The queen was born in 69 B.C. to Ptolemy XII Auletes and his queen, Cleopatra V. There is absolutely no evidence whatsoever that she was illegitimate and none to suggest her mother was an Egyptian, all the more so since one now recognizes the mutual antipathy the Macedonian Greeks and Egyptians shared for one another. To attempt to identify the ethnicity of this queen on the basis of a citation from Shakespeare or by referring to a painting by Michelangelo is scientifically unsound. Shakespeare's plays, although they may rank as great works of literature, are, nevertheless, classified as fiction, not history.

As a Macedonian Greek descendant of the family of Ptolemy I, the dynasty's founder, Cleopatra VII nevertheless understood the greatness of Egypt's past, doubtless because she alone of the members of her dynasty could read and understand the hieroglyphs. Cleopatra was certainly present at Edfu when the inaugural ceremonies were performed by the high priest of the falcon-god Hor, by which the best preserved of all Egyptian temples today was officially consecrated and opened for worship. Her ability to read the ancient Egyptian language revealed to her firsthand the accomplishments of the divine wives of Amun and granted her access to information about the careers of such elite members of Egyptian society as Hatshepsut and Nefertari. She, too, like Rameses II wondered where the glory of Egypt had gone. Growing up in Alexandria she watched how her mother and father were divided in their opinion of how to rule the country. She witnessed the success of her mother's faction which drove her father into exile. She understood the importance of Rome, because she saw how her father was able to enlist Roman money and Roman soldiers, enabling him to return to Egypt, drive out her mother's faction, and assume control of the reigns of government once again. The commander of those Roman forces was none other than Mark Antony (pages 204-205).

In 51 B.C., upon the death of her father, Cleopatra was elevated to the throne of Egypt. She was destined at first to rule jointly with her half-brother, an expedient dictated by her father before his death in an effort to avert the continuance of the familial political feud. Her father's plans were aborted, however, when her brother, Ptolemy XIII, managed to gain the upper hand, forcing Cleopatra VII to flee Alexandria.

By happenstance, Julius Caesar was then engaged in a civil war against Pompey, whose forces he had routed at Pharsallos in Greece. With nowhere to turn, Pompey decided to seek safe haven in Egypt, but almost immediately

By the first century B.C., Egypt and Rome were the two world superpowers. Cleopatra VII inherited the throne of Egypt in 51 B.C.

upon arrival in Alexandria he was seized by the agents of Ptolemy XIII and beheaded. Julius Caesar, in swift pursuit, docked shortly thereafter and was presented with Pompey's severed head; Ptolemy's agents thought that their dastardly deed would stand them in Caesar's favor. Much to their surprise, he was sickened by the sight, maintaining that even his worst enemy was not worthy of such inhumane treatment.

A quick study of the situation revealed to Caesar that Cleopatra VII ought to be the rightful ruler of Egypt, because he judged her, and rightly so, to be better trained, educated, and equipped to rule than her brother. As hostilities between the two camps escalated, Ptolemy XIII died by drowning. Cleopatra VII was now made queen of Egypt, serving as co-regent with her younger brother, Ptolemy XIV, who posed no threat to her reign.

Contrary to Hollywood and the playwrights, Cleopatra VII was not the sex kitten of one's imagination. She was the political and intellectual equal of Julius Caesar, and together with him plotted the domination of the known world. It is for that reason, and that reason alone, that she accompanied him to Rome where he installed her in luxury. Because she was queen of Egypt, Cleopatra VII could claim to be a goddess, and the goddess with whom she identified most was Isis, whom the Romans had equated with Aphrodite. Aphrodite was, according to Roman mythology, the goddess from whom the Romans themselves sprang. In a very manipulative way, then, Julius Caesar was implying that his alliance with Cleopatra VII was linking Romans with their mythological ancestor. Cleopatra the Great played the role to the hilt – together they could aspire to world domination. She even bore him a son, Caesarion, which means "little Caesar".

These regal aspirations of Julius Caesar, as one well knows, were his downfall because they led to his assassination in 44 B.C. Cleopatra VII was left without an ally, and was forced to return to Egypt in order to pursue her dreams. These dreams could only be attained, or so it seemed at the time, if she was able to align herself to yet another powerful, like-minded Roman. That Roman soon surfaced in the person of Mark Antony, whose acquaintance Cleopatra VII had made earlier when he accompanied her father back to Alexandria. Mark Antony was now himself engaged in a power struggle against Octavian, Julius Caesar's nephew and adopted heir. Antony was intrigued by the possibilities of an alliance with Cleopatra and thought that he would use her resources to further his own ends. How wrong he was. History has shown that Cleopatra VII, and not Antony, was the dominant partner in this relationship.

The combined forces of Antony and Cleopatra VII challenged the Roman forces of Octavian until the two fleets stood oar to oar at Actium in Greece.

T-shirts are today. Over this is a long skirt, wrapped around the body so that its fringed side comes to rest directly between the legs. A fringed shawl is then draped asymmetrically over the body leaving one shoulder exposed. The shawl is held in place by the left hand.

Ancient Egyptian texts suggest that the linen from which such garments were woven was extremely costly and that only members of the upper echelons of the elite could afford to wear them. This is, therefore, an ideological statement as much as a fashion statement. Although created very late in the history of Egyptian civilization, Hor still professed his adherence to those moral and ethical qualities for which the ancient Egyptian elite is justly famous. Here is what he has to say about himself in that regard in the inscriptions on the back pillar (detail, right): *[I am one] who protects the pauper from the wealthy, the one whose hand is swift for the widower... who correctly performs that which you [the pharaoh] wish, the one who speaks the truth and acts justly...* In return for such behavior and because of his demonstrable piety toward the gods of Egypt, the text proclaims the following: *This statue [of Hor] is established in the presence of thee,* [a deity, whose name is lost due to a lacuna, or gap, in the inscription] *in order that its name might be pronounced upon the earth forever...* That piety paid off in the end. Today, almost two thousand years after this statue was made, visitors are still pronouncing the name of its owner, Hor.

Statue of the Official Hor
(detail of back pillar, right)
**Late Period/Late Ptolemaic
to Early Roman Period
Gray granite; 33 3/4" in height
From Alexandria; CG 697**

This very interesting statue was found in Alexandria and represents an official, Hor by name, who was probably active as a priest of Thoth, god of wisdom, at the time Cleopatra VII was ruling Egypt. Earlier scholars attempted to dismiss his costume as non-Egyptian in origin and style, but recent investigations have shown that the costume represents a typically native Egyptian fashion which gained currency during Dynasty 26. It consists of three garments. The first is a T-shirt designed exactly the way

had on these other groups and intentionally redoubled their efforts on behalf of those cults in an attempt to distance themselves further from others. Such veneration was an effective means of keeping strangers at arm's length, in keeping with the xenophobic nature of that elite. This Buchis Stela was dedicated by Ptolemy V Epiphanes, the Macedonian Greek ruler of Egypt, who is shown in adoration before the Buchis bull. Ptolemy V Epiphanes is also commemorated on the Rosetta Stone. The kind of inscription, therefore, that Champollion had to deal with when deciphering the hieroglyphs can be appreciated, since this stela is written with the same style of hieroglyphs and for the same pharaoh as that famous monument. It was the identification on the Rosetta Stone of the cartouche, or ring, containing the hieroglyphs for Ptolemy's name, that helped break the code.

Statue of a Roman, perhaps Mark Antony, in the guise of an Egyptian
Late Period/Ptolemaic Period
Black basalt; 37 3/4" in height
From Mendes; 10484/5

This statue falls within the definition of ancient Egyptian art as symbolic rather than representational. Any attempt to compare the features of its face with the likeness of individuals from other cultures is methodologically unsound, comparable to likening the proverbial apples with oranges, because the Classical artists sculpting images of Greeks and Romans are far removed from the ancient Egyptian craftsmen, who were co-opted by the elite to make manifest ideology. Nevertheless an identification may be proposed because of the way in which the Egyptian craftsmen employed insignia and attributes as visual clues. The nemes-headdress, for instance, lacks the uraeus, an indispensable insignia of pharaohs. The nemes without a uraeus would suggest that this individual is connected in some way with the position of pharaoh, but is not himself pharaoh. The hair on the forehead, protruding from under the nemes, is not Egyptian in style, but it does recall the hairstyles of Romans, particularly in the way the locks form the so-called "crab's claw" on one side. The Egyptians were capable of imitating just about anything they saw, but rendering it in accordance with their artistic conventions (pages 130-131). This hair is rendered in precisely that way. The visual clues provided by the statue, therefore, suggest that a foreigner, perhaps a Roman, associated with the position of pharaoh, is here represented. Julius Caesar is excluded because of his baldness. Octavian, later Augustus, is excluded because of his decidedly anti-Egyptian stance. Caesarion, the son of Julius Caesar and Cleopatra VII, is excluded because he was assassinated at an early age. The only viable candidate, then, is Mark Antony, who was a Roman, stayed in Egypt long enough to have statues of himself in pharaonic style erected, but who was never permitted by Cleopatra VII to assume the trappings of kingship. For these reasons, there is a very good possibility that this statue may be a representation of Mark Antony in the guise of an Egyptian.

Stela of the Macedonian Greek Pharaoh Ptolemy V Epiphanes offering to the sacred Buchis Bull
Late Period/Ptolemaic Period
Painted limestone; 26 7/8" in height
From Armant; JE 53143

Despite their non-Egyptian origins, the Macedonian Greek rulers of Egypt, in order to ensure the status quo, engaged in several displays of piety toward the native Egyptian gods. Such acts included the reverential mummification and interment of the sacred animals throughout the land. In contrast to some cultures, which hold that all animals of any given species are sacred, the ancient Egyptians habitually selected one and only one living beast which, in any given locality, might be considered a manifestation of that site's principal deity. The veneration of specific bulls falls into this category, but it must be noted that the bull was considered a manifestation of several different deities, including the god Ptah at Memphis, as the Apis Bull, and Re at Armant, near Thebes. The bull at Armant was anciently called either the *living ba [life force] of Re*, or *the soul over the deceased*. When this last epithet was pronounced in ancient Egyptian it sounded to the ears of the Greeks something like "buchis", hence the traditional modern designation of that animal as the "Buchis Bull." The cult was thoroughly reorganized during Dynasty 30 and the faithful continued to worship, install, and bury Buchis bulls right through to the very end of the Roman Imperial Period. The persistence of this veneration in the vicinity of Thebes over such a long period deserves comment. The Greeks, Romans and Christians were appalled by the Egyptian practice of worshipping animals in this form and repeatedly expressed their revulsion to such practices in no uncertain terms. The members of the Egyptian elite realized the effect their worship

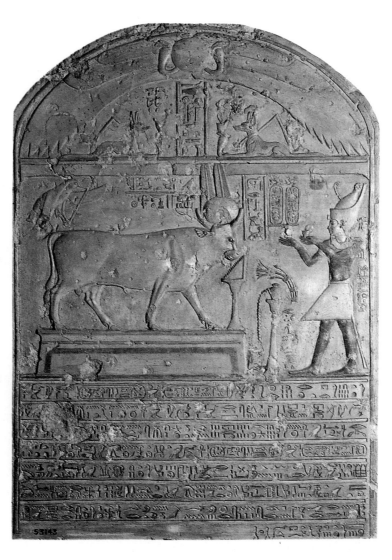

The Roman occupation of Egypt
after the suicide of Cleopatra VII was
accompanied by major cultural
dislocations. Memphis no longer
played a dominant role in the political
life of the country, partly because
Augustus had effectively curtailed the
power of the Memphite elite and
partly because the administrative hub
of the country was now firmly
established at Alexandria.
Nevertheless the country had to be
controlled in order for the Roman
government to benefit from taxes and
revenues. To that end, the Romans
decided to erect a fortress alongside
the River Nile where, it has been
suggested, a ferry connected the road
linking Heliopolis to Memphis.
To this day, such a direct road still
exists and one can take it directly
from the airport to this very site.
For reasons which are still obscure,
the Romans named this site Babylon,
although it appears to have no
connection, however remote, with the
more famous city of Babylon on the
Euphrates River.
During the course of the late first and
early second century A.D., initially
under the administration of the Roman
Emperor Trajan, the complex was
either enlarged or completely rebuilt.
The Roman Empire peacefully
merged into the Byzantine Empire as
a result of the transfer of the capital of
the empire by Constantine the Great
from Rome to Byzantium, which was
renamed Constantinople in his honor
and dedicated in A.D. 330. That
single act also renamed an empire,
and placed Egypt squarely in the lap
of its eastern provinces.
The Byzantines appropriated many of
the fortresses erected by the Romans,
and Babylon was no exception. It was
here at Babylon that Amr ibn al-As,
leading the forces of Islam, chose
to test the military capabilities of the
Byzantines. And it was here that
Cyril, the Byzantine Greek Orthodox
Patriarch and governor, stood in
the final days before the fortress
finally capitulated to the terms of Amr
ibn al-As. These events occurred in
the winter of A.D. 639, and resulted
in the introduction of Islam to the
African continent.

The outcome of the battle of Actium in 31 B.C., known in the annals of warfare as the last naval battle of the ancient world, dashed Cleopatra's hopes. She realized that there was no accommodation with Octavian, of whom it had been remarked, "when you die, Octavian, you will have been the only mortal to have done so, without having first lived." As a result, the queen resolved to commit suicide and convinced Antony to do the same. He botched his attempt, and was dragged, mortally bleeding, into the queen's presence where he eventually expired. Cleopatra, on the other hand, chose to end her own life with dignity and grace. When Octavian finally managed to enter her chambers, he found her body as if she were asleep.

The method she chose for her suicide is not known. Tradition maintains that she fell victim to the venom of an asp; some claim it was the venom of two serpents; and others suggest that she pricked her delicate skin with a pin, the point of which had been laced with deadly poison. She was apparently buried within the city of Alexandria, but the exact location remains a mystery.

Following Cleopatra's death, the triumphant Octavian fostered a smear campaign to discredit her and those associated with her, while promoting his own cause. Those propaganda attacks accused the queen of being an enchantress who used her feminine wiles to seduce such noble Romans as Julius Caesar and Mark Antony. In fact, the queen was monogamous and faithful, both to Caesar, bearing him one son, and to Anthony to whom she bore twins. She was not the licentious creature of Hollywood movies.

The Romans, notorious for their misogyny, posthumously ridiculed Cleopatra for taking her own life. The Roman poet Horace put it this way: *Bold enough to regard her fallen realm with a straight face/ and yet mighty enough to grasp savage serpents/ so that her body might drink of their black venom,/ she was egged on by her vicious determination for suicide/ and without any regard whatsoever for the arriving Roman fleet/ this woman, far from being humble, dashed our hopes of leading her/ through the streets of Rome in triumph/ by taking her own life in a most unladylike fashion.* Had Cleopatra VII been a Socrates, or any other man, her suicide would have been admirable, but such behavior for women, at least in Roman eyes, was out of character for their gender.

Octavian's treatment of Cleopatra's children was dictated by his political inclinations. As a result, he ordered the assassination of Caesarion who, as the flesh and blood child of Julius Caesar, could press a greater claim to being Caesar's heir than could Octavian, who was only a nephew and an adopted son. On the other hand, her children by Mark Antony fared much better. The daughter, Cleopatra Selene, grew to adulthood and married Juba II, king of Mauritania, situated within the territory of the modern nation state of Morocco.

Octavian, who as Augustus became the first emperor of the Roman Empire, did visit the Alexandrian tomb where he beheld the mummified body of Alexander the Great. Having had his fill of that vision, he was asked whether he would also like to view the Ptolemies, to which he curtly replied, "I have come to behold a god, not a bunch of dead bodies."

However, Augustus was so fearful of an opponent rising up against him from the soil of Egypt that he decreed the nation to be the private property of the imperial family. Romans could only visit after obtaining a visa issued and signed by the emperor himself. He wanted the world to know that he had conquered Egypt and was in control as neither the Assyrians nor the Persians before him had been. To demonstrate his power, he ordered the removal of an ancient Egyptian obelisk from Heliopolis to Rome. Now known as the Monte Citorio obelisk, it was reerected in the Campus Martius where it served as a gnomon, or indicating rod, of a giant sundial. The political overtones were unmistakable because the Egyptian sun god, to whom the obelisk was related, was now made a subject of Apollo, the Roman sun god.

Try as he might, Augustus was not able to eradicate the attraction which Egypt held for the Romans of his day. Many villas in the Italian south, particularly at Pompeii, were decorated with scenes inspired by ancient Egypt, and the elegiac poet, Propertius, writing during the reign of Augustus, praised Isis and her cult in his poetry.

As time passed, more and more Roman emperors, regarding themselves as the masters of the civilized world, realized that only Egypt, of all ancient civilizations, rivaled the grandeur of Rome. Members of the Egyptian elite realized this predilection on the part of the Roman emperors and played it for all it was worth, openly declaring their willingness to collaborate with the agents of those emperors. For the time being, at any rate, the members of the Egyptian elite seemed to benefit immeasurably from such cooperation.

The Roman Emperor Nero was among the first to take an active interest in ancient Egypt, partly because he himself was a distant relative of Mark Antony and wished to set the record straight. So, for example, he ordered the Roman prefect, or governor, of Egypt, to clear the sand away from the great Giza Sphinx, and ordered his legions into Africa to identify the source of the Nile. The members of this mission reached Khartoum in the Sudan and reported the discovery of what we now identify as the White Nile, in the process presenting the emperor with a rhinoceros. Nero is even said to have had his wife, Poppea, mummified and buried according to Egyptian rites.

The Roman Emperor, Domitian, ruling in the second half of the first century A.D., was no less enamored of things Egyptian. He decided that he was in fact divine while alive, and based that divinity, in part, on his acceptance of the divinity of the pharaohs of ancient Egypt. As a result, the monuments he created at Beneventum, a town in southern Italy not far from Pompeii, were adorned with numerous statues of himself in the guise of the pharaohs of old, replete with kilts and nemes-headdresses, as well as with statues of sacred Apis bulls and at least one version of the sacred barque of the goddess Isis.

No Roman emperor, perhaps, was more blatant in his love of things Egyptian than Hadrian in the second century A.D. During one of his tours of inspection throughout the Eastern territories of his realm, he chanced to visit Egypt. There his beloved, the comely Antinoos, committed suicide by drowning himself in the River Nile. He did so, he said beforehand, in order to fulfill a prophecy and so avert any harm from falling directly upon Hadrian himself. Hadrian was so taken by this selfless act of devotion that he found a brand new city, Antinoe (Sheikh Abada), on the bank of the River Nile opposite the spot where the drowning took place. On his return to Rome, he commissioned certain members of the Egyptian elite to create a hieroglyphic inscription in honor of Antinoos. That text was eventually inscribed upon the Monte Pincio obelisk, now in Rome's Viale del Obelisco.

Soon the traditional way of life, enjoyed by members of the Egyptian elite for over four millennia, was about to change abruptly, and that change, some have argued, was unintentionally self-inflicted.

With Octavian's conquest of Egypt in 31 B.C., so began over three hundred years of Roman rule. The Roman emperors recognized Egypt's importance as a civilization to rival their own, and the Egyptian elite exhibited once again their unerring ability to accommodate a foreign invader.

Statue of an enthroned official
Roman Imperial Period, A.D. 25-50
Basalt, with inlays; 19 1/2" in height
From the Faiyum; CG 1191

The costume worn by this male official is a variant of that worn by Hor (page 204), the shawl of which is secured at the neck by what appears to be a round clasp. The eyes have been inlaid. The two inscriptions are both in Demotic, a very abstracted form of the hieroglyphs. They were added later at different times. The inscription on the side is problematic and translates as follows: *Psais and his brother and wife and children.* Psais apparently decided to appropriate the statue by adding his name together with a mention of the rest of his family. There is also a depiction of a camel (detail, left) on this side of the throne.

The inscription on the front claims that the statue was erected on behalf of the Roman Emperor Tiberius, as an offering to a relatively obscure deity, Pakysis, by one Hor, a common name of the period. This inscription is clear evidence of the way in which members of the Egyptian elite attempted to curry the favor of their Roman overlords. By honoring the Roman Emperor Tiberius, and linking that honor to the cult of an obscure, local god, Hor hoped to secure his advantaged position.

The fact that the statue was usurped is important, because it suggests that by the time of the early first century A.D. the manufacture of statues in pharaonic style had virtually ceased. As a result, this statue may profitably be regarded as one of the last statues ever made in ancient Egypt for an elite member of its society.

The statue is of further interest because it demonstrates how long-lived ancient Egyptian traditions were. One need only compare this statue of Hor to that of Iris (pages 56-57), crafted about 2,500 years earlier, to understand visually how conventions formulated by the elite were maintained and passed on from generation to generation. Both statues depict members of that elite as enthroned figures in a statue type originally developed for the representation of pharaohs (page 49). And yet they are so close to one another in design and conception that they can be taken as proof of just how conservative and traditional that society was.

CHRISTIANITY AND ISLAM

Previous page
**View of the ruins of the Coptic
Monastery of St. Jeremiah
Fifth century A.D., Sakkara**
Of all of the sites one can visit in
Egypt today, none affords such a
panorama of ancient Egyptian history
as does Sakkara. From the tombs
of the Archaic Period (pages 28-29)
down to the Christian Period,
represented here by the Monastery
of St. Jeremiah, a visitor with time
can explore monuments from virtually
every epoch of ancient Egypt's four-
thousand-year-old history.
The Monastery of St. Jeremiah
occupies an area upon a flat ridge
below the rise immediately to the east
of the Tomb of Horemheb (pages
152-153). Tradition maintains that it
was founded late in the fifth century
A.D., at a time when the Copts,
as the Egyptian Christians are called,
had split from the Byzantine
Greek Orthodox Church in order
to maintain their adherence to the
Monophysite doctrine regarding
the nature of Christ.
The establishment of such a
monastery here in the desert of
Egypt brings back memories of early
anchorites. Those individuals
abandoned their lives of comfort
in towns and villages, and fled to the
deserts. There they endured hardships
and solitude in order to devote
themselves to more spiritual pursuits.
Monasticism, as practised in the West,
was born here in Egypt in just such
communities. It is no coincidence,
therefore, that St. Anthony of the
Desert, a saint from Egypt, maintains
a preeminent reputation as just such
an anchorite. And if St. Anthony
might have been tempted by
the devil to abandon his prayers
and meditations in order to return
to civilization, the ancient Egyptian
tombs in the desert, such as that
of Horemheb, which is not far away,
may have been regarded as the source
of that evil temptation. After all, the
walls of that tomb are decorated with
scenes which include the deceased
seated in comfort before tables laden
high with offerings of every kind.
In the eyes of these anchorites such
depictions represented all that
they had renounced in their struggle
to maintain a spiritual life.
The Monastery of St. Jeremiah was
rebuilt time and again as the Christian
community grew and prospered.
It was finally destroyed in the tenth
century A.D. by the Muslims, whose
initial conquest of Egypt in A.D.639
was welcomed by the Copts.

The members of the Egyptian elite, in an effort to safeguard their advantaged station in life at all costs, developed the habit of throwing in their
lot with whichever foreign invader happened to be around. Indications of
this habit are already clearly visible during the Hyksos occupation of the land,
and the same pattern of behavior has been seen time and again as the Assyrians,
Persians, Macedonian Greeks, and Romans took control of the country. In the
process the members of the elite were apparently so anxious to cooperate with
the foreigners that they paid very little or no attention at all to the plight of the
remaining 90% of the population. During the course of the Roman Imperial
Period, the members of this elite, growing smaller in number each year, stead-
fastly maintained contact with both the agents of the Roman emperors in Egypt
and very often, as has been seen, with the emperors themselves (pages 208-
209). The Roman emperors rewarded them handsomely for their cooperation
and the elite, now ensconced in ever smaller communities, primarily in Upper
Egypt, lived an ivory-tower existence. They were of the firm conviction that
nothing would change, because their way of life had endured for so long.

Such a complacent outlook on life failed, however, to take into account the
realities of the day. The Roman emperors, far removed from Egypt in distant
Italy, were not members of the elite, the way the pharaohs had originally been.
Their immediate political, social, religious, and economic concerns were not
the concerns of the elite. As the Roman emperors attempted to assert themselves throughout their empire, they met with resistance. There were any
number of cultural groups within the Roman Empire who refused to recognize
the divinity of the Roman emperor and worship his cult statues. That number
included, but was not limited to, the emerging Christian communities and
certain members of the Egyptian elite. Roman agents took drastic measures in
an effort to coerce those who refused to embrace the cult of the Roman
emperor into doing so.

In Egypt there is no more visible record of this type of Roman coercion than
the architectural modifications to Luxor Temple. The Romans realized that
ancient Egyptian cults functioned because, during the festivals regulated by the
religious calendar, specific divine barques of particular gods had to travel in ritual
procession along prescribed routes to goddesses resident in other temples. These
processions began and ended along the main axis of the individual god's temple.
In those processions, the way into and out of the inner sanctum was always along
that principal axis; there was no possibility of a short-cut in the form of a right-
or left-hand turn. And so it came to pass at Luxor Temple that the Romans
intentionally blocked the processional way by throwing up a wall in front of the
inner sanctum, effectively strangling the circulation of such religious processions.
The wall was then equipped with a niche into which a cult statue of the reigning
emperor was placed. Because the cult statue was facing the temple's entrance, it
was literally, figuratively, and metaphorically intended to mean that the Roman
emperor himself was turning his back to the Egyptian deity of Luxor Temple.
The Egyptian elite, who had so excessively relied upon the Romans for their well-
being, were now repudiated by those very individuals.

It has been suggested in this context that the group of statues initially discovered in the so-called Luxor Cachette (pages 108-111) were intentionally buried
by the last pagans before these architectural modifications were effected in
Luxor Temple, in the hope that they would be able to return the statues to their
original locations once the Roman threat had passed. Moreover, the members
of the elite could not turn to the remaining 90% or so of the population for
support, because the members of those agrarian masses, realizing that they had

been abandoned by their own priests, turned elsewhere for religious solace, namely to Christianity.

According to Judaeo-Christian traditions, many Biblical events are associated with Egypt. Accordingly, the Christian Holy Family fled the wrath of King Herod by seeking refuge in the land of the Nile. The identification of the places mentioned in that account with actual locations in Egypt remains problematic, but those same traditions maintain that the Coptic Church of SS. Sergius and Bacchus in Old Cairo is built over the site, provided with water, where the Christian Holy Family stayed during its sojourn in Egypt. This Church is only minutes away on foot from the Jewish Synagogue of Ben Ezra, which Hebraic tradition maintains marks the spot where pharaoh's daughter pulled Moses out of the bull rushes.

St. Mark is said to have arrived in Alexandria about A.D. 60, after which time the Christian community in Egypt grew. Their persecution during the reigns of the Roman emperors Decius and Diocletian was so severe that the Egyptian Christians, the Copts, mark the beginning of their own religious calendar with the year A.D. 284, when such persecutions first occurred. Persecuted by the Romans and ignored by the more advantaged members of their own society, is it any wonder that this abandoned people embraced a religion which extended to them a modicum of hope in an otherwise hostile environment?

Christianity spread rapidly in Egypt. Documents relating to the early Church fathers provide an exceptional window on the landscape of the Christianization of Egypt. During the course of the fourth century A.D., particularly after the Edict of Milan, Christianity was no longer a proscribed religion; the edict guaranteed individuals the freedom of choice in matters of religion. The Christians could now practice their religion without fear of reprisal. As time passed, more and more pagan Egyptians were converted to Christianity. The elite members of society, whose numbers were steadily decreasing, continued to worship the pagan gods. As a result, the members of the Christian community, which included both secular and clerical officials, started to harass the pagans.

One poignant incident is illustrative of the process. A pagan temple had been wantonly destroyed by a group of zealous Christians. They had acted illegally, but since the civil authorities were also Christian no charges were brought against them. Some time later, a pagan Egyptian, who was a member of the elite, attempted to celebrate the rites of the gods in the ruined temple. He was not breaking any laws. Nevertheless, a crowd of Christians gathered in order to force the pagan to desist from worshipping the gods of his choice. They had the complicit backing of local Christian magistrates. The Christians apparently justified such actions, which could be construed as peaceful retaliation against the pagans for the years of earlier bloody persecutions wrought by the pagans against their forbears. Such acts seemed to occur with increasing frequency during the course of the fourth century A.D. until the edicts of the Emperor Theodosios closed all pagan institutions throughout the empire. For all practical purposes Christianity was the official religion of the day, as practised in the Eastern Orthodox rite of Byzantium, from which city the Byzantine emperors now ruled. These edicts hastened the death of pharaonic civilization, because the temples and cults with which the members of the Egyptian elite were most associated were now proscribed. As a result, a way of life which had dominated the land of the Nile more than four millennia was aborted. As the last temples closed forever, and the few remaining ancient Egyptian priests died, the secret of the hieroglyphs was lost. It was to take almost two thousand years for scholars to learn once more how to read and write that language.

With the destruction by the Romans of the very fabric of their ancient religion, the Egyptian people turned increasingly to Christianity. A way of life that had endured for over four millennia came to an end.

The Copts — Egyptian Christians — believed in the single nature of Christ, and consequently broke away from the Byzantine Greek Orthodox Church.

The remaining pagan priests finally converted to Christianity, and, like the Egyptians who had converted before them, are called Copts, a name derived from a corruption of the ancient Greek word for Egypt, [ai]gypt[os]. Their language, Coptic, is really the spoken ancient Egyptian language, but written with letters of the Greek alphabet together with a handful of other letters derived from Demotic. This phenomenon can be compared to the way in which the letters of the Greek alphabet were modified in order to write certain Slavic languages in the Cyrillic alphabet. Although originally a vernacular, the Coptic language today is generally reserved for liturgical purposes within the Coptic Church.

In 641 A.D. Egypt came under Muslim rule; the Copts welcomed the Muslims as their liberators from the Byzantines.

The Copts are Monophysites. That is, they believe in the one nature of Christ. They are still a thriving minority in modern Egypt and rely on their own pope for spiritual guidance. In the 1970s the Church of Ethiopia came under the authority of the Coptic Pope, or patriarch, whose traditional seat is in Alexandria, where St. Mark first preached Christianity. As Monophysites, however, the Christian Egyptian Copts adhere to a doctrine about the nature of Christ which was fundamentally different from that of the Byzantine Greeks, the official rulers of Egypt during the early centuries of Christianity. A rather complex picture then emerges, because the native Egyptians, as Christian Copts and Monophysites, found themselves ruled by co-religionists, the Byzantines, who advocated the diophysite doctrine regarding the nature of Christ.

These differences escalated into heated debates, resulting, in A.D. 451, with the Ecumenical Council of Chalcedon, a city in the modern nation state of Turkey. The overwhelming majority of Christian prelates in attendance voted to adhere to the diophysite doctrine of the Byzantine Greek Orthodox Church. According to this doctrine, Christ's divine and mortal natures are separate. As a consequence Christ, the diophysites would argue, was able to perform miracles, suffer the Passion and die on the cross. That decision so alienated the Egyptian Copts that they immediately severed their relations with the mother church of Christianity and went their own way. They worshipped in their own churches (pages 214-215) and maintained religious congregations separate and distinct from those of the ruling Byzantines.

In time the Byzantine Empire was challenged from the East by the forces of Islam. Egypt, then a province of the Byzantine Empire, was finally attacked in A.D. 639 by the Moslem general Amr ibn al-As, who served under the Caliph Omar, one of the four immediate successors of the Prophet Mohamed. In July of the following year he surrounded the Byzantine stronghold of Babylon (not to be confused with the more famous city of the same name in Iraq). The Byzantine Emperor Heracleios, through his representatives in Egypt, could offer but limited resistance, and the fortress capitulated in April of 641. Amr ibn al-As then marched on Alexandria, gaining control of the city as a result of a treaty. The Copts of Alexandria welcomed the Muslim forces, which had rid them of their proselytizing Byzantine overlords. As a result, the Muslims allowed the Copts to elect their own patriarch, Benjamin.

The Muslim conquest of Egypt was neither harsh nor violent. They allowed the Byzantines ample time to clear up their affairs and move out. In the process, a great many valuable items found their way to Byzantium. Among the treasures were many books from the famous library of Alexandria. Proof that these books were transported to Byzantium comes in the form of inventories which were compiled in Greek afterwards, and which record in minute detail the contents of the library and the order in which its great librarians had followed one another. As a result of such documents, no one can claim that any one disaster destroyed the contents of the library. It was simply, as one scholar put it, "borrowed to death," when the removed scrolls were not returned.

From such beginnings, Islam took root on the African continent, and was to grow. The city of Cairo played, and continues to play, a major role in that growth. Today, as one looks at the Islamic monuments in Cairo, such as the mosque of Mohamed Ali (pages 220-221), one cannot help but recall Islam's glorious past. This citadel was refortified by Salah al-Din, whom the West calls Saladin, and who will forever be linked to the Crusades and the adventures of Richard the Lion-hearted. Islamic Egypt is filled with such glorious traditions, and Egypt, led by Cairo, still remains the undisputed leader of the Arab world in many different fields of endeavor.

Overleaf
View of the Citadel at sunset
Ninth century A.D., Cairo
Babylon capitulated to the forces of Islam, led by Amr ibn al-As, in A.D. 639, and their camp became the site of the first Islamic settlement from which the city of Cairo was to grow. That early community, called Fostat, still exists under that name as a Cairene district. About two centuries later, Hatim, a governor of Cairo, realized that the heights on which the present Citadel stands enjoyed the benefit of cool breezes which might relieve the intense heat of summer. He therefore erected a pavilion, or resort, on the hill which he appropriately named The Tower of the Winds. There is some debate as to whether this really was the first structure on the hill, because certain scholars have suggested the existence of an earlier, but by that time abandoned, Roman garrison. Be that as it may, The Tower of the Winds remained a popular retreat until it was destroyed by members of a rival Islamic dynasty, who regarded it as a symbol of their defeated foe. The hill remained deserted from that time until 1167 when Salah al-Din (Saladin), descended from a Kurdish family, emerged as ruler of an Islamic Empire with capitals at both Damascus and Cairo. Upon becoming sultan in 1171, he inaugurated the building of a defensive wall around what is now Cairo. The fortification of the Citadel was a strategic component of that defensive system. Salah al-din is, of course, justly famous in the West for his participation in the Crusades, but few realize that this defensive project was built with the toil and sweat of a workforce composed almost exclusively of captured Crusaders. Today, the dominant feature on the Citadel is the Mosque of Mohamed Ali, which is traditionally referred to as the Alabaster Mosque because of the stone with which its walls are veneered. The mosque contains the tomb of Mohamed Ali, who was born in Kavalla, a city now in the modern nation state of Greece, not far from Thessalonika. Mohamed Ali began his illustrious career as an officer in the Ottoman army, commanding a regiment composed of Albanian Muslim soldiers. This is not the place to discuss Mohamed Ali's spectacular rise to power, other than to mention an armed revolt against the Ottoman authorities and the premeditated assassination of 470 individuals who were invited to the Citadel to participate in a celebration and were shot to a man as they approached the gates. In time, Mohamed Ali declared his independence from the Ottomans and became the founder of a dynasty, whose last member was King Farouk. King Farouk was ousted from power in 1954 by a military coup from which General Abd al-Nasser eventually became the first native Egyptian since Pharaoh Nectanebo II of Dynasty 30, almost 2,000 years earlier, to lead the Egyptian people. Mohamed Ali is buried within this mosque which bears his name.

INDEX